# Blind Ambition

## By Ever Lee Hairston

Houston, Texas * Washington, D.C.

Blind Ambition © 2015 by Ever Lee Hairston

Brown Girls Publishing,

LLC www.browngirlspublishing.com

ISBN: 9781625179159 (ebook)

ISBN: 9781625179166 (print)

# Dedication

To my 95-year-old mother: Arizona Hairston;

My siblings: Roger Hairston, Rosie Bethea, Verona Bell
and Clarence Hairston Jr.

Of course, my only son: Victor Hailey

Dedicated friends,

The entire National Hairston Clan, Inc.

And

My National Federation of the Blind Family

*"My mission in life is not merely to survive, But to thrive; And to do so with some passion, some compassion, some humor and some style."*
*-Maya Angelou*

Growing up, I faced many disappointments, which greatly diminished my self-confidence or perhaps shadowed my self-esteem. But I had to learn that we may encounter many defeats but we must not be defeated.

Through everything that I've endured, I believe that my life has a purpose. I have had to learn to love myself and honor myself as I am.

I know that honor, self-respect and self-love are crucial to happiness. I have forgiven others because holding onto resentment, anger, and hatred only hurts me and robs me of my life's joy and happiness. It is also important to forgive myself. Regret is an appalling waster of energy and I cannot throw away my happiness on guilt or shame.

Therefore, I have gratitude for all of life because gratitude unlocks the fullness of life and turns what we have into enough and more. It turns denial into acceptance and turns chaos into order.

Gratitude makes sense of my past and brings peace for today and creates a vision for tomorrow. So, I have made the choice to be constantly grateful for all of life.

Thanks to my family (Biological family and Federation of the Blind Family); To my friends and acquaintances, I have been so fortunate to meet over the years; and especially to God for love, hope and determination.

I hope you enjoy my story.

*Ever Lee*

# Chapter 1

I can hear my mother's voice as if it were yesterday.

"Ever Lee!"

No matter where I was -- upstairs in my bedroom, downstairs in the front room, or even playing with my brothers and sisters out front, I always heard my mother calling me.

"Ever Lee! Get me some eggs."

Even though gathering the eggs that the chickens had laid was one of my chores, I always dreaded it. But there was no way I would disobey my mother. So when she called, I did what I had to do.

It always felt like such a long walk to the kitchen. To get there, I had to walk across the squeaky planks of the back porch from one side of the house to the other. The kitchen was on the opposite side from where I slept and the kitchen was where the chickens laid their eggs -- right beneath the floor. That was why some of the floor planks were left loose...so that all you would have to do was reach down and grab the eggs.

But for me, there was only one problem with that.

Snakes!

I was really scared of snakes. Whenever one got anywhere near me, I would take off, running as fast as my legs would take me. That's why I dreaded getting the eggs. Because if the eggs were under the house, there could be a snake down there, too.

But even though I was afraid, I still had to do what my mother told me. So, I would go to the center of the kitchen and stand over the loose plank, then lift it up. My hands were always shaking as I held the plank with the tips of my fingers. Crouching down, I would get low enough to put my hand beneath the floor, but I was still high enough so that I could make a run for it if I saw a snake.

Most of the time, though, I was able to get under the house, get those eggs, drop down that plank, and give the eggs to my mother -- all without being attacked. But doing that chore was always so stressful.

I'd been afraid of snakes and any kind of rodent all of my life. But snakes and rodents were just a part of living on a plantation in the country.

That's where I lived...on a plantation. I was born on the Cooleemee Plantation, which was in the western part of North Carolina. The plantation was just one of many that was owned by the Hairstons, who were originally a family from Scotland. And during the 1600s, 1700s, and 1800s, the Hairstons were one of the richest slave-owners in the country, with plantations throughout North Carolina, Mississippi, and Virginia.

By the time I was born, the owners of the Cooleemee Plantation where I lived were Miss Elma Hairston and her son, Judge Peter Hairston, III. Miss Elma was a widow; her husband, Peter had passed away a few years before I was born.

The Cooleemee Plantation may have been in the Hairston family for generations, but it was also where my ancestors had lived for just as long. Even though slavery had ended many, many years before I was born, my family was still there -- my grandparents and parents were part of what many called the new slavery...they were sharecroppers and we all lived there on that land.

While my grandfather and grandmother worked in the fields, their primary responsibilities were in the plantation house, taking care of Miss Elma and her family. Back in the day, my grandfather, William Thomas Hairston, would've been called "the house nigger," but when I was growing up, most people had stopped using that term -- at least in public.

My grandfather did a little bit of everything for the Hairstons, serving their needs; Tending and cultivating the vegetable garden, "beating the biscuits daily," which was a ritual and churning the butter. While he did that, my grandmother, Ruth (who everyone called Charmin) did most of the cooking. Then, after a long day at the plantation house, my grandparents would return home to their log cabin, which was on the plantation, too. And it was there where they raised twelve children, the seventh one being my father, Clarence.

My father and his siblings had to work hard growing up, doing all kinds of chores like taking care of the farm animals, gathering firewood (which we used for heating and cooking), planting and plowing the fields, and even getting out there in the fields during the season and picking cotton, gathering corn and wheat.

It was a life of long days and hard work, which is probably why all of my father's brothers and sisters grew up and moved away. Every single one of my aunts and uncles migrated to bigger cities in North Carolina, and some even moved far away to the North. But, wherever they went, they all left -- except for my father.

I never knew why my father stayed behind. Maybe he knew that someone had to look after his parents and he just took on that responsibility. But, he stayed on Cooleemee and built his own life.

He met my mother, Arizona, in church and just a few years later, they were married. My parents had seven children: Roger, (who we called Wence) Rosie, and then, I came third. Right after me, was my sister, Rebecca. She and I were very close, primarily because I felt it was my responsibility to take care of her. Rebecca was a sickly child who had to have several surgeries growing up and I always did what I could, whenever I could to make her feel better. Rounding out our family was Mary Louise, Verona, and Clarence, Jr. who never lived in the log cabin like me and the rest of my siblings. Clarence was born in the new house that we moved into in 1952.

With all of those children, my mother and father, and my grandparents, we had a full house. And a full house is a perfect way to describe it because that log cabin wasn't very big.

It was built like two small houses really, with a huge chimney in the center that separated both sides. One side was where my grandparents stayed and on that side, there was the kitchen, one bedroom upstairs and one bedroom downstairs.

To get to our side of the cabin, you had a choice. You had to go outside, but you had to walk across the huge front porch or the back porch that connected the two sides. Once you got past that chimney, you entered our side of the house with the living room (though, we didn't have any living room furniture in there) and then there was a huge room upstairs where we all slept. My parents slept in one bed with whoever was the youngest, and then, me and all my other siblings slept in the other bed. The only one who didn't sleep in that room with us was my older brother, Wence. He slept on the other side of the house with our grandparents.

I loved being around my family. It was a lot of fun for us kids because had each other to play with. But while I loved my brothers and sisters, there were things that I just didn't like about the plantation. I didn't like that we didn't have any of the modern conveniences. We didn't have running water, and we didn't have indoor plumbing. Instead of a bathroom in the house, we had an outhouse. Going to the bathroom was as scary as getting those eggs from under the house.

The outhouse was about three hundred yards behind the cabin and even though my father kept the grass cut and cleared of weeds, there was always a chance that I was going to see a snake.

It was so scary, but it wasn't just my fear of snakes that made me so afraid of the outhouse. I couldn't stand the smell. When you got close, you could smell the stench of all of that waste rising up from the earth. I'd try to hold my nose and not breathe, which was impossible, of course. But I would hold my breath as long as I could. As bad as that smell was, though, it still wasn't as bad as what would've happened if I'd seen a snake.

Whenever I had to go out back to the outhouse, I'd hold my breath, and then move as fast as I could. And once I got in that wooden shack, I never sat down on that bench that housed the latrine. I just stooped down low enough to take care of my business and then I would get out of there.

Not having running water wasn't as bad as not having indoor plumbing. For our water, we had to wind water from the well, and fill up buckets for everyone to take their baths. We'd also filled up buckets for cooking and drinking and it was the water that we used for drinking that made me turn up my nose. We'd put a dipper in the drinking bucket and then when someone wanted a drink, they'd scoop the dipper into the water, take a sip, then put the dipper right back in. There was no way to rinse the dipper off, so it wasn't clean at all.

When I went to get a drink, I would always

hesitate, stare and study that water, just to make sure there wasn't anything floating around in there. With everybody in that house, there were too many people using that dipper. And especially my grandmother, who dipped snuff. I was always afraid that some of her snuff would end up in my water.

My mother always got on me when she saw me standing there trying to decide if I was going to get a drink or not.

"Girl, that water is not going to kill you," she'd shout at me.

I wasn't so sure of that. How could it be healthy to drink behind my grandmother and everybody else like that? But if I was thirsty enough, I would drink out of that bucket.

It was a very simple life for us. For my parents, everything was about work and taking care of their children. My father worked in town at a variety of factory jobs, my favorite one being when he worked at Colbert Ice Cream. I loved the ice cream and the dry ice that my father brought the ice cream home in. That dry ice gave me and my brothers and sisters lots of hours of fun.

No matter where my father worked, though, he always came home to more work in the fields: plowing and planting and then, during harvest time, he'd pick the corn, peanuts and of course, the cotton. As a sharecropper, he and my grandparents worked the land for a 70-30 split – 70 percent going to the plantation owners. I could never get myself to understand how, when my family was doing all the work, they got the lesser share. As I got older and really began to understand the inequality, it made me angrier. But that was just the way it was back then. It wasn't like my family could negotiate a better deal.

As children, our lives were as simple as my parents and grandparents. We all had our chores: feeding the chickens, picking the peanuts, digging the potatoes, hauling the firewood, drawing water from the well, and during harvest time we had to pick cotton. It didn't matter how old we were -- if we could walk, we could work.

And, I just didn't like any of it! I didn't want to do that kind of work. I didn't want to feed the chickens, I didn't want haul firewood, and I especially didn't want to pick cotton.

That was one reason why I loved school so much. When I was at school, I was far away from the plantation. But beyond that, I just had a genuine love for learning. I got my love for school from my grandfather.

Born in 1875, my grandfather wasn't formally educated; he was a self-taught man. From as early as I could remember, my grandfather would read the newspaper every day, and I would watch as he sat there learning about everything that was going on in the world. As I got older, I would read the newspaper with him and that pleased him. My grandfather respected education, and he knew the possibilities and opportunities that opened up because of education.

Of course in the South during that time, I only had the opportunity to attend segregated schools. From the first grade to the third, I attended St. John's Elementary, which was a three mile walk to and from school every day. Then, in the fourth grade, I went to Cooleemee Elementary. Cooleemee was about eighteen or nineteen miles away from the plantation, so we had to get up extra early and take the bus, passing several white schools along the way.

Cooleemee was a brand new school, though it was very small. There were only five classrooms, plus the nurses' office that also served as the business office, and a cafeteria that was also the auditorium. Add to that the kitchen and two restrooms, one for the girls, one for the boys. And that was our whole school. But it was fine since there were less than one hundred students and only five teachers.

But even though it was small, and even though it was segregated, I loved it. I loved everything about learning. I loved being challenged, loved being exposed to things that I'd never heard before. And I especially loved reading. I loved all kinds of books, the subject didn't matter to me. And, it didn't matter that at our school the books were hand-me-downs from the white schools. As long as there were pages, as long as there was something to read, as long as there was something to learn, it was good enough for me.

Reading was just another way for me to get away from the plantation. Not physically, of course, but in my mind. Inside the pages of a book, I could escape to other places, I could dream about places where I'd never been. I could imagine places that didn't have outhouses and snakes and loose planks on the kitchen floor. Places where I wouldn't have to feed the chickens and pick peanuts and haul firewood. Places where I could just go to school and learn and never have to worry about work or living on a plantation.

There were times when our house and the plantation came alive. In 1952, the summer before I entered the fifth grade, Miss Elmer and Judge Peter built us a new house, still on the plantation. It was a bigger house; now my parents had their own bedroom, the girls had their own bedroom and the boys had theirs.

But the best thing about the new house was when the holidays came -- especially Thanksgiving and Christmas. Of course, all of my father's siblings came back to the plantation for holidays before we moved. But once we were in the new house, I really remember all of those good times.

With everyone home for the holidays, our house was really crowded, busting at the seams. So that everyone would have somewhere to sleep, we set up pallets everywhere: in the hallway, in the kitchen, even under the dining room table. No matter where you looked, you would see a Hairston. You could hardly walk on the floor without stepping on someone. It was crowded, but it was fun. We just made it work.

And we made eating work the same way we made sleeping work. Even with all of those people in the house, we had formal sit-down holiday dinners in the dining room. Because of our large family, we had a huge table, but it only sat twelve. So during the holidays, we ate in shifts. One group would sit down, talk, and laugh, and eat, and then, when they were finished, we'd clean the table, wash the dishes, and set the table for the second seating. Then, more adults would sit down, talk, and laugh, and eat. We just kept going until everyone ate.

Of course that meant that the children ate last. But that didn't matter to us. It was never a problem because there was always enough food. Sure, sometimes the potato salad or the vegetables would be gone. But my mother always made sure we had something, even if it was just chicken feet. My mother could fry up some chicken feet. Those chicken feet would taste so good, just as good as the turkey that the adults ate.

I loved those holiday times and when everyone left, we returned to our lives. But there was a moment in time when I was able to get away from the plantation. A moment that I thought was going to be so great, but it didn't quite turn out that way.

# Chapter 2

The summer before I was going into the fifth grade, my aunt and uncle, who lived in Durham, North Carolina told my parents that they wanted me to come live with them so that I `could go to school in the city.

"She's really smart," my Aunt Charmin and Uncle DeEdward told my mother and father. "Going to school in the city will be a great opportunity for Ever Lee."

Out of all of my siblings, my aunt and uncle chose me. Can I tell you how honored I felt?

When my parents first told me that I was going, all I could do was think about what my life was going to be like in Durham. The best part was going to be living in their house that was nothing like our plantation house. With my aunt and uncle, I'd share a room with my younger cousin and since they had indoor plumbing, there would be no outhouse! That meant, there wouldn't be any snakes, and I wouldn't have to do any of those chores -- like drawing water from the well or feeding chickens. And there wouldn't be any cotton to pick. I couldn't wait to go.

That September, a few days before school started, I packed my bags and said goodbye to my parents, my siblings and the plantation. I didn't know what to expect, whatever was in front of me was going to be so much better than what I was leaving behind. Not only the house, but school, too. I knew that the school would be far better than my school in the country. I'd be in a larger building, have better teachers and I'd probably even have new books!

I was just so excited.

But, it wasn't long before my excitement turned to horror. It only took a few days of being in that school for me to realize just how far behind I was. And I was behind in every area.

First, there were the academics. Sitting there in that classroom, I sometimes felt like I was in a foreign country. I couldn't understand what the teacher was saying, I wasn't able to answer questions, I couldn't solve any of the problems. I just had a very hard time keeping up.

Then, I had a challenge with my speech.

Some said that I had a lisp, others said I was tongue-tied, no matter what, I sounded "country" compared to the city kids. So, I was pulled out of my class once a week, and taken away from the other kids so that I could have speech therapy.

Being taken out of class like that was pretty embarrassing, and only added to my hardship of trying to fit in. Socially, it was as much of a nightmare for me as it was academically. The children in the city were not welcoming, they were not friendly and I felt so alone. The kids didn't reach out to me and they didn't make it easy for me to reach out to them. It was bad enough that I already felt different, but those kids made sure that I knew I was different.

Maybe it would've been better if I'd had time to bond with the kids, but there was no time to do that. Back at home, we rode the bus to school, so we had time to hang out with the other kids before and after classes. But in the city, I lived only a few blocks away from the school. So, like everyone else, I walked -- by myself. That left me feeling isolated and lonely. And, it left me vulnerable to my first bully.

I hadn't even been at the school for very

long, probably only a few weeks when a girl in my class, walked up to me right before I got to the lot that I had to cross to get to the school.

"What're you doing?" she asked me.

I didn't know how to answer that since I wasn't doing anything except walking to school. And surely, she could see that.

When I didn't answer, she said, "Give me some money." Just like that.

Why did she want money from me? I didn't ask her that, though, because just the way she asked for the money, kind of demanding it, made me pretty scared. "I don't have any money."

She marched right up to me and her face was only inches away from mine when she growled, "You better give me some money or I'm going to get you."

Before the last word was out of her mouth, I took off. I ran so fast, not looking back and not stopping until I was inside the school building. I didn't even breathe until I was inside and safe, just so grateful that I'd gotten away from her.

Except, I didn't get very far away because the next day, she was waiting for me again, right at that lot. And just like the day before, she walked up to me, got in my face and said, "Give me some money."

My voice was shaking when I told her the same thing that I'd told her the day before, "I don't have any money."

"I'm going to get you," she said.

And, just like the day before, I took off. This went on for days. She'd walk up to me, she'd demand money, and I'd run away. After a few days of being threatened by her, I found out that her name was Maxine. I had no idea why she'd chosen me to threaten. I had no idea why she thought I had money since I didn't have a penny. If I'd had anything, I would've given it to her. But since I had nothing, I just kept running.

If I'd been back in the country, I would've told somebody what was going on. If not my parents, I could've told Wence or Rosie. But, I was in the city by myself. And, I didn't want to tell my aunt and uncle. I didn't want to disappoint them in any way and I certainly didn't want them to send me back to the plantation.

So, I stayed quiet. In the mornings, I ran away from Maxine and at night, I cried. My tears weren't just about Maxine, though. I cried because living in Durham was just so hard. I was only ten years old and I didn't know how to handle not having any friends. I didn't know how to handle not being one of the smartest kids in the class. I didn't know how to handle feeling so alone.

I didn't think that it could, but after a couple of weeks of being bullied by Maxine, things got worse. One morning, she came up to me like she did every day, but this time, she changed it up a little.

"Give me some money," she demanded.

"I don't have any money."

This time, though, she didn't say her usual, 'I'm going to get you.' This time, she said, "If you don't give me some money, tomorrow I'm going to beat you up."

Before, I'd been scared. Now, I was terrified.

Beat me up? Just because I didn't have any money? I had no idea what I was going to do. I'd never been in a fight. I didn't know how to fight. All day long, I couldn't even concentrate in class. All I could think about was getting beat up. I thought about that at school, I thought about it when I got home, I thought about it while I did my homework and ate dinner.

I thought about it so much that when I went to bed, I hardly slept. By the time morning came, I was exhausted and just resigned to the idea that today was the day. I was going to have my first fight. I was going to get beat up for the first time.

Although I knew I was going to get beat up, I wasn't trying to rush to the fight. I took my time eating breakfast, I took my time walking to school. But just like she'd been doing every morning, Maxine was waiting for me.

"Give me some money," she demanded.

My heart was pounding so hard, my chest began to ache. "I don't have any money," I said, fighting to keep my tears away.

And just like she promised, she hit me. Now, like I said, I'd never been in a fight. But just because I'd never fought before, didn't mean that I was just going to stand there and let her beat me up. So, when she hit me, I hit her back.

I guess my working on a plantation -- lifting those buckets of water, running after the chickens, hauling firewood into the house -- had helped me because it only took a couple of seconds before everyone could see that I was stronger than her. And, I was winning the fight.

By the time it was over, I had beaten her up. All of that time, I'd been scared for nothing. My bully situation had been solved. But that was the only thing that got better in school. Everything else stayed the same...I was just so unhappy.

I didn't feel that way all the time, though. Every so often, my parents would drive up to see me and when they came with my brothers and sisters, those were the best days. The first time they came was in November, and I got to meet my new little brother, Clarence, who was born just a month after I left for school. Not only was I excited to see the baby, but I was excited just to be sitting around with my family and listening to them tell me everything about what was going on back at the plantation. I soaked up all the stories that my siblings told me about school and church. For someone who didn't want to be at the plantation, I sure wanted to know about everything I was missing.

While those were some of the best days, those were also some of the worst nights. Because eventually, my parents and brothers and sisters had to leave. Those were the nights when I cried the most. It was so ironic -- I had wanted to get away from the plantation, but it wasn't until I was away that I realized the plantation was where I really wanted to be. Because while I hated that we didn't have a modern house, and I had to do a lot of chores, I realized that it was on the plantation where I had a lot of love. It wasn't that my parents were affectionate or expressive. It was just that once I was away, I could look back and see how they loved me. I wouldn't have even been in Durham if they didn't love me and want the best for me.

Of course, I knew that my aunt and uncle really loved me, too. They would've never invited me to live with them if they didn't. They were giving me the opportunity to live up to the potential they saw in me and that was love.

But the thing was, I didn't fit in in Durham. I belonged back on the plantation.

Looking back, I'm not sure that I really understood all of that at that time. But subconsciously, I knew it. And my body began reacting violently to the stress that I was under. It started with headaches, terrible headaches that made me throw up, headaches that no one -- not my aunt, not my teachers -- understood. I understood them, though. The headaches came because I was holding my emotions inside. I never told a soul about all that I was going through. No one knew that I was struggling, academically and socially. No one knew that my heart was breaking. No one knew that I was terrified of disappointing my aunt and uncle and parents and grandparents. No one knew at all, that I was under so much stress.

It was the headaches that let my aunt and uncle realize that maybe Durham wasn't the best place for me.

I would've never asked to go back home, so when near the end of the school year, my aunt and uncle decided for me. I was so excited. Who would've ever thought that I would be happy going back to Cooleemee? But, I was. The end of the year couldn't come fast enough. I couldn't wait to go home.

# Chapter 3

It was good to be back home.

One of the places that I'd missed most when I was away in Durham, was my home church. Not only was my father a deacon, but so many of my uncles and cousins were ministers. So a big time for us was the revivals. That was when all the ministers from all over would come to our church. And then, dinner would be at our house. Having all of those people there for the revival was just like the holidays. Our house would be packed from the doors to the walls with people, and my mother, grandmother and aunts would be in the kitchen cooking for all of these people. We were always ready for guests, there was always enough food. My parents and grandparents kept one-hundred pound bags of pinto beans, and huge bags of cornmeal. With the chickens in the backyard, and all the ham we had in the smokehouse because we raised hogs, we were always ready and able to make a meal.

While my mother and grandmother did most of the cooking, all of us kids had chores that we had to do to help get ready for the ministers and church members who would be coming to our house to eat. My chore would be to get a chicken. As soon as my grandfather said, "Ever Lee, go out there and kill a chicken. We've got to have food for them," I would head to the backyard. I'd learned how to do this from my grandmother when I was very young. So by the time I was eleven, I could do it by myself.

My mother or my grandmother already had the huge black pot set up for me. They'd have the pot set over the fire and the water would be boiling by the time I went out to get the chicken. The chickens were all in the backyard and all I had to do was grab a chicken by his legs and as soon as I held him, then, I'd wrap my hands around his neck. The chicken would be squawking, but his noise didn't bother me. I would swing the chicken around and around until I'd finally wrung his neck off. All I had to do was drop the now headless chicken, even though it continued jumping and running around even without its head. Eventually, of course, it would stop moving altogether. Then, I would pick up the dead chicken by its legs and very gently and carefully dip it into the boiling water. That loosened the feathers on the chicken so that they would be easier to pluck. And once that was done, I would take the chicken into my mother. She would fry it up, and we'd all have a good meal.

Those were some of the best times for me at church, but it was also when I returned from Durham that I had responsibilities at the church. I had to speak for the Baptist Training Union and for the Usher's Convention. My father would take Rosie and I to the Usher's Convention every year and I loved to go because they had a speech contest every year. When I was older, my father put me in as one of the speakers.

I was so excited to be going, but I was nervous about having to speak. The topic that I had to speak on was Why am I a Baptist? I knew that I would do well with that. But there was a scary part to this for me as well. I was afraid about the stage. Would there be enough light for me to see? Would I stumble or fall and embarrass myself?

Well, I didn't stumble and I didn't fall. I was able to walk up onto that stage and stand at the pulpit and give my speech about why I was a Baptist.

And I won! My first public speaking engagement ever, and I did it! Little did I know that was going to be the beginning of me speaking in front of hundreds, and really thousands of people. I loved doing it then and these speeches were going to serve me well later. Between the revivals and going to the church conventions, I was really happy to be back home. And I was just as happy to return to my school. Yes, Cooleemee Elementary wasn't as good as the school in Durham. But, it was better for me. Yes, my school was smaller, and was filled with second-hand books, but I fit in here. The teachers cared about me and I had friends. It was a different life, but a life that was better for me.

At Cooleemee, the teachers really cared about me. I felt the difference the moment I came back to school. I returned to the plantation in time to go into the sixth grade with Mrs. Mohawk who was a very compassionate person and my favorite teacher.

I knew it then, but looking back, I saw all that she'd done for me. She was always challenging me to go beyond my comfort zone. And she made learning so much fun. Every day I felt like I was discovering something new.

When she realized how much I loved to read, she gave me a book to take home and read. It was a book about New York. I can't recall the name of the book now, but it felt like a treasure to me. The book was all mine and I was so happy about that since we didn't have any books at home. My parents were so busy working and taking care of us, they didn't feel that purchasing books was a priority.

In seventh grade, I encountered my second bully. It was hard to believe because before I had gone to Durham, I hadn't gotten into any fights. But, here I was back at home and a girl was ready to fight me again.

It had started innocently enough. My seventh grade teacher, Ms. Dalton knew my family well. I think that's the reason why she would send me on all kinds of errands. She knew that I came from an honorable and respectable family and so when she needed something from the store, I was the one she would send.

One day, she sent me to the store to buy some facial tissues, and this time, she sent one of my classmates, Burtha, with me. The General Store wasn't far away; only about three blocks. So, Burtha and I walked.

Well, when we got to the store, I headed straight to the section for the tissues, but Burtha went to the candy section. After I picked up the box of tissues for Ms. Davis, I came around the aisle, and I saw Burtha putting candy right into her pockets.

I didn't really think she was going to steal it, but after I paid for Ms. Davis' purchase, Burtha followed me right out of the store. All the way back to the school, I thought about what Burtha had done, but I didn't say anything to her. I didn't say anything until we got back to the school.

After Burtha went back to her seat, I told Ms. Dalton what happened. "Burtha stole some candy."

I was really surprised at her reaction. I expected her to be upset, but she didn't seem like she was. She just kinda nodded a little, smiled, and all she did was give a little hum, "Uhmmm."

It was as if she already knew.

I didn't see Ms. Dalton say a word to Burtha, and I thought maybe she'd forgotten about it. But she must've said something, because the next day, Burtha came up to me and said, "I'm gonna beat you up."

All I could think was, 'Oh, no! Here we go again!' What was with all these girls who wanted to beat me up? And if I thought it was bad in Durham, it was really bad this time.

First of all, I was really scared of Burtha because she was really mean to most of our classmates. I knew she could fight. And then, not only did she keep threatening me every day, but she got some of the other girls in the seventh grade to join her and gang up on me.

This was worse than in Durham because at least with Maxine it was just her. But this time, it was Burtha and these other girls. I was just miserable.

And it was hard to stay away from Burtha. Not only were we in school together, but we rode the same school bus. Her stop was the last one before we rode to the school and for the last twenty to thirty minutes of the bus ride, Burtha tormented me. Every day she'd remind me that she was still going to get me, she was still going to beat me up.

Finally, the day came when she decided we were going to fight. And just like the last time, I stood up for myself. I knew I had to -- if I didn't defend myself, Burtha would always come after me. And just like the last time, Burtha hit me and I pushed her so hard, she fell to the ground. That was the end of the big fight. There were no more threats from her and no more fights.

But it wasn't just the bully that changed my life in the seventh grade. There was always a lot of work to be done on the plantation and now my responsibilities expanded to the fields.

For the first time, I had to stay home and pick cotton.

There was a season for chopping-cotton -- two weeks in the Spring and then, picking-cotton two weeks in the Fall. During those two weeks, I worked side-by-side with my older siblings chopping and picking cotton. It was always horrible, not only because it was hard work, but because I hated missing school. I knew being out of school wasn't good -- I would definitely fall behind.

But, even though I knew the importance of my education, my parents only concern was getting the work done. And now that I was old enough, I had to be out there with everyone else.

Those cotton-picking days were hard, long days. We'd get up early in the morning and go out to the field where there would be mile long rows of cotton. It was always so hot with the sun bearing down and no shade anywhere around. I'm sure sometimes it was over one hundred degrees.

I carried a cotton sack around my waist, and would have to bend down to pluck out the cotton boll that had blossomed out of the boil. It wasn't always easy to get the cotton because often, it was sticky and would cling to my fingers. So, I had to take my time. That meant it would be hours. Hours of picking. Hours of walking up and down and working every row.

Of course, while I was out in that field picking cotton, I would be on the lookout for snakes. We were out in the open, so, I knew snakes were out there, too.

We worked until the sun started to set and

then in the morning, we would be back out there. Long, long days for two weeks straight.

There were some days when I got lucky. There were days when I didn't have to go into the fields, but I still wouldn't go to school, either. I had to stay home to watch after my younger brothers and sisters. That was easier than being in the field, but looking after my siblings wasn't easy. My sister, Rebecca, was always very sickly, and not only did I have to look after her, I had to look after Mary Louise, Verona, and Clarence, Jr, too. While Wence and Rosie were in the fields, I had to get the kids up, get them dressed, cook for them, and then keep them occupied for the whole day.

This might sound like I didn't want to work, but that's not what it was. When I had to work, but didn't miss school, I felt better about it.

That's why I liked working at the plantation house. I was in the eighth grade when I began helping my parents and grandparents when Miss Elma and Peter had parties. They would have these huge, grand parties where lots of people would come dressed up and I would help my parents serve their guests. I was the only one of my siblings who worked these parties with my parents.

I worked hard and Miss Elma noticed because she gave me a job. It wasn't any kind of a full time job of course. I went to school every day, so, I could only work for Miss Elma on Saturdays. But for four dollars a day, it was great. I did cleaning, mostly, sweeping the large front and back porches, making the beds, and cleaning the bathrooms. I liked cleaning the bathrooms the best because believe it or not, that gave me a chance to read.

Besides the book that Ms. Gaither gave me when I was in the sixth grade, we didn't have any other books. But there were books at the plantation house. The first time I cleaned one of the upstairs bathrooms, I noticed the library in the room right next door.

The library belonged to George, one of the Hairston children, and he had shelves and shelves filled with books. I would save that bathroom for last, then take my time cleaning. After I made sure that no one was nearby, I would duck into the library, grab a book, then run back to the bathroom, closing and locking the door behind me.

Once I put down the cover to the toilet seat, sat down, and then tucked my legs up to my chest, I would read for as long as I could. That was such a treat for me.

But a bigger treat came when one Saturday, I asked George if I could take one of his books home to read. I'm not sure what made me ask him. I guess I wanted to have the chance to finish reading the whole story that I started.

"Sure," he said. "But I have to ask my mom first."

When George came back and said that his mother, Mrs. Lucy said yes, I was really excited. Now, I'd have a book to read at home!

At this point, I was the only child working in the plantation house. My older sister, Rosie, had worked in the house at one time, though she wasn't paid as I was. She just babysat the Hairston children.

But Rosie hadn't worked there very long because Miss Elma discovered that my sister couldn't see very well. The children would throw balls around the house and when a ball rolled under one of those very high poster beds, my sister would run to try to find it, but she would never find that ball.

What no one knew at the time was that my sister couldn't see in the dark or in dark places. When Miss Elma found out, she didn't know how serious my sister's condition was. All she knew was that she didn't think it was a good idea for Rosie to take care of the children anymore.

My parents took Rosie to our family doctor and she was prescribed glasses. What no one knew at the time, was that I suffered from the same Eye Disease (Retinitis Pigmentosa or RP), an inherited degenerative eye disease.

And soon that disease would affect me and every part of my life.

# Chapter 4

The eighth grade was a very interesting year for me.

Again, I had another teacher in my life who took a great interest in me. Right at the beginning of the year, Ms. Marks said, "Ever Lee, you love to read. I want you to be in the Spelling Bee. You're going to represent the school."

I was so excited! Me, in the Spelling Bee? I couldn't wait to get home and tell my parents. But when I got there, no one was as excited as me.

I told my mother first. "Mom, I'm gonna be in the Spelling Bee at school!" I said excitedly.

"That's nice," she said without even looking at me. "Now make sure you go get your chores done."

That was all she gave me. But as my mother stood at the stove, I guess I could understand that. My mother was busy taking care of the family. She didn't have time to think about

47

education and because she'd only graduated from the seventh grade, I don't think she ever saw the importance of it. Maybe it was because she worked on the plantation and she didn't see what education was going to give her.

But even though I was a kid, I knew education was going to be my way of having a better life.

It was hard to find anyone at home to be excited with me about the Spelling Bee.

Rosie was a good speller, however it was hard because it was getting more difficult for her to see. And my dad wasn't home -- he worked all the time.

So, it was just me.

At school, I practiced with Ms. Marks. And then when I got home, I studied myself. I took those words everywhere with me. When I had to do my chores, whether I was feeding the chickens or picking peanuts, I kept my notebook with me. I practiced pronouncing words, and then spelling them at the same time.

Even when we sat down to dinner, I would have my notebook because I wanted to use every single moment to study.

But when my mother saw what I was doing, she got upset. "Ever Lee, you better not do that at this table!"

I was really hurt and disappointed by that. All I wanted was my mother to be proud and to be supportive of me. But once she told me that, I had to study in secret. There were times when I felt so alone at home.

But back at school, I felt alive again. Ms. Doland was so encouraging. And not only about the Spelling Bee. Ms. Marks pushed me to get involved into all kinds of activities at school. She made sure that I signed up to be in the glee club.

I never did participate in that Spelling Bee. I just wasn't prepared for it. But it meant a lot to me that Ms. Marks believed in me that much.

While eighth grade was a big difference for me academically, things changed for me socially in the ninth grade.

It was in the ninth grade when I decided that I wanted to be a debutante with one of the sororities in Salisbury, NC. The idea of going to charm school in Salisbury, North Caroline was the thing that intrigued me the most about doing it. Just from what I knew about the debutante pageants, I knew that I'd become more sophisticated. But being a debutante meant finding a way to raise the money I'd need.

There was no way my parents were going to be able to help me with this. First of all, we didn't have a lot of money to begin with. But with my sister, Rebecca being so sick, a lot of my parents' money went to take care of her.

So, I went to two of my aunts -- the one who lived in Durham and another aunt who lived in Winston-Salem. Both of them were excited that I wanted to do this and said they would help me.

My aunt in Winston-Salem helped out by finding me a job. My aunt told me about a family in Lexington who needed a babysitter for their two children, a four-year-old and a toddler. I was excited to meet the Smith family and I worked for them during the summer. Then, during the school year, I would actually take off from school on some Fridays, so that I could watch the children.

At first, I really liked being with the Smiths. Ms. Smith was a nurse, and I loved watching her and talking to her about her work.

But while I really liked Ms. Smith, I wasn't so

crazy about Mr. Smith. Being around him sometimes made me uncomfortable. He didn't say much to me, but every now and then, I would catch him staring at me. And, I hated when I was left alone in the house with him. That happened every morning. Ms. Smith left the house before he did, and I couldn't wait for him to be gone.

Then one day, right after Ms. Smith left, I heard Mr. Smith calling out to me.

"Ever Lee!" he shouted in his thick, Southern drawl.

At first, I didn't know where he was. But he kept calling and calling until I figured out that he was in the shower.

I stood far outside his door. "Yes, Mr. Smith."

"Bring me some soap," he shouted.

Bring him some soap? I said to myself in my head. It didn't make sense to me, but what was more important was that I really didn't trust him or what he was asking me to do.

So, I leaned a little closer to the door. "Mr. Smith, what did you ask?"

"Bring me some soap," he repeated. "It's in the kitchen, under the cabinet. Just bring me some soap."

My heart started pounding right away and all kinds of thoughts were going through my head. This is not right, I told myself.

"Bring me some soap!" he shouted out again.

I didn't know what to do. As I was trying to figure it out, I grabbed the soap from the kitchen cabinet, then walked slowly toward the back of the house. But, I had made up in my mind that if something happened, if this went down the way I thought it was going to, I was going to run.

"Mr. Smith," I called when I got right to the outside of the bathroom door. I reached inside the bathroom to hand him the soap. The soap dropped and when I leaned over to pick it up, Mr. Smith grabbed my hand.

I knew it! I knew that's what he was going to do. I jerked my hand away from him and ran back into the living room, snatched my handbag off the couch. I wasn't worried about him following me. First of all, he was naked and the children were in the house. But still, I got out of there and ran all the way to my cousin Gwen's house. And that wasn't a short distance. Gwen lived three miles away.

But at least I'd earned some money. I kept working on the plantation, too, so that I could be a debutante. And I loved that time. The sorority sent me to charm school and I met other girls away from Cooleemee. It was a good time.

And it was a good time in school. I was really involved in high school. From being a cheerleader on the basketball team, to being on the school Glee Club, I tried to do as much as I could. I even worked in the Principal's office. Being involved in so much really helped me to become well known and popular. And the icing on the cake was when my classmates elected me to be the May Day queen. I'd earned the respect of my peers and they made me the queen of the school.

\*\*\*

One of the things that I loved to do with my family was take short trips to visit relatives who lived beyond the Cooleemee Plantation. One of my mother's sisters lived in Lexington and often, Rosie and I would go with our mom to see her. My aunt had had two children, a boy and a girl, though the girl died when she was young. But I loved seeing my cousin Henry. He went to Dunbar High School and I was impressed with that. I looked at Dunbar as a better school than our school in the country. Dunbar had a football team and that was so cool.

We were at my aunt's house one day, when I was in the tenth grade and Rosie was in the twelfth, and Henry introduced us to his friend Samuel who lived next door.

"Samuel is the quarterback at Dunbar," Henry told us.

Boy, was I impressed.

"You know what you two should do?" Wade asked us. "You should come and see us play next weekend."

We have never been to a high school football game before and we were so excited. We were even more excited when our mother said it was okay for us to go. So we made plans to come back to Lexington the next weekend and go to the game.

All week long, I thought about Friday night. The football game was going to be exciting enough, but afterward, Samuel was going to drive us all to the Do-Drop Inn, a really popular place where teenagers hung out. Then, we would stay overnight at my aunt's house.

When Friday came, we went to Lexington, and met up with Samuel and Henry. On the school grounds, Samuel pointed out where he wanted us to meet after the game.

"I'll be parked right here," he said before he ran off to the locker room to get ready.

Rosie and I held hands as we walked into the stadium and found seats on the bleachers. It was as exciting as I imagined it would be. We sat on the side with all of the Dunbar students and we cheered right along with them. By the time the game was over, I was a little hoarse from all of the cheering, but the night was not over. I was looking forward to going to the Do-Drop Inn almost as much as I'd been looking forward to the game.

It wasn't until we stood up that Rosie and I noticed just how dark it was. The lights in the stadium had been so bright, it felt like it was still daylight. But as we made our way down the bleachers, it was completely nighttime.

"We'll be all right," Rosie said as she held

onto me. "We just have to walk down this street."

She was right; we just had to walk down one street, but it was a long sidewalk, about three hundred yards from the stadium. As we walked, I noticed the signs and cones indicating construction was being done on the sidewalk, but I couldn't make out the words. I didn't bother to ask Rosie; I knew that I could see better than she did.

We walked slowly, feeling our way down the street, when suddenly, we both took a step and fell, landing inside a deep hole.

Both of us screeched out, first, by our surprise, then with our fear.

"Are you okay?" I asked my sister.

"Yeah. But what happened? We just fell into a hole."

"Yeah."

It was hard for us to see anything and I had no idea what we were going to do. So, we began calling out for help. But even though we yelled, no one came to our rescue. We knew there were people walking by, but no one stopped. No one did anything to help.

I wasn't going to stay down in that hole much

longer.

"We've got to climb out ourselves," I told Rosie.

The climb was steep and hard since we'd fallen into a dirt hole. We kept getting half way up and falling back down. I dug my heels in, and being taller and a little more agile than Rosie, I was able to finally make it up to the top. Then, when Rosie got half-way up, I reached down, and pulled her out with me.

We were in shock for a moment, as we stood there, not believing what had happened to us and not believing that no one had come to help.

"What happened to you?" Samuel asked us when we finally made our way to where he and Henry were waiting for us.

I could imagine how we looked, covered with dirt. I told him how we'd fallen and how no one had helped us.

"Maybe they thought you were kidding," Henry said.

I had no idea what it was. And to this day, I'm still baffled by that. By the time we got to the Do-Drop Inn, all Rosie and I wanted to do was get into the bathroom and clean up. That was an experience that I will never forget.

But while I had these good (and some not so good) times in high school, high school was also the time when I began to seriously think about my future. It was in my junior year in high school when I started thinking about what I wanted to be, what I wanted to do with my life. I knew I was going to leave the plantation -- I just didn't know how.

But one day when I was with my sister, Rebecca, I realized what it was that I wanted to do. One day, I saw Rebecca run into the backyard and my heart sank. Because whenever she did that, she was sick.

Rebecca was born with a liver disease that she had her whole life. And it just didn't seem like anyone knew how to care for her. But when I saw her run into the backyard, I knew she was going back there to throw up; she would always throw up blood.

I ran out of the house, too, but I ran the other way. We didn't have a telephone, so we always ran to the plantation house to get someone to drive Rebecca to the hospital.

I think Ms. Elma got so used to it that when

she saw one of us running like that, she knew what to do. She would just call out, "Lucy!"

Lucy Hairston was Ms. Elma's daughter-in-law. She was married to Peter, and everyone in our family really liked Ms. Lucy. She didn't treat us like Ms. Elma and Mr. Peter. Ms. Lucy treated us well, like we were all equal to her.

And she would always help us when she could. As soon as she heard her mother-in-law call out, she would come running. And then, she would help me get Rebecca into the car.

Ms. Lucy had this down to a science. Before she left with Rebecca, she would call the police, who would send the Highway Patrol. So, all she'd have to do was drive to the main highway, and then the patrol met her there. The Highway Patrol would then drive Rebecca fifty miles to the nearest hospital.

Watching Rebecca that day, I really wished that I could help my sister. And watching her that day let me know what I wanted to do.

I decided then that I was going to be a nurse!

I knew a couple of nurses. My Aunt Charmin in Durham was a nurse at Duke University and then, there was Ms. Smith in Lexington. I knew that my aunt would help me.

Making that decision made me feel really good. Because for the first time, I was starting to believe that I had a real way off of the plantation. I felt like I was planning for my future and being a nurse was going to be the perfect way out.

I really started seriously thinking about becoming a nurse when I was in the twelfth grade. But it wasn't anything that happened with Rebecca or anything that happened in school that made the difference.

It was picking cotton.

There were few things that I disliked more than picking cotton and one day during the Fall season when I was out there with my brother Wence, and my sister Rosie, I kept telling myself that this cotton picking really wasn't for me.

We were working on a plantation where hundreds of acres of cotton were planted. We started picking that cotton and about fifty yards down the cotton row, I leaned forward to pick this beautiful cotton out of the cotton boil. But when I looked down, right there in front of me, lying on the ground was a long, black snake. I screamed.

"What's wrong with you?" Wence asked.

"There's a snake. I can't do this!"

"That one little snake ain't gonna hurt you. We have to do this, we have to finish picking this cotton."

I'm not sure how Wence convinced me, but he did, and I kept on picking. But then, about twenty yards down that cotton row, I went to pick another cotton ball, and right on the ground, there was a brown snake.

I screamed. And then, I saw another snake and another one. Snakes were all around me. I didn't stop screaming and I took off running. My brother and sister were right behind me. We ran as fast as we could and didn't stop until we reached a trailer parked at the beginning of the cotton row. But, I was so frightened, I didn't stop even then. I climbed the very top of that trailer and sat on one of the sacks stuffed with cotton.

I sat there, scared, out of breath, and crying. "I can't do this anymore," I whispered to myself. "I just can't. There's got to be a better way."

I kept telling myself that over and over. And I knew right then that I was going to find my way out.

# Chapter 5

That snake changed my life!

I'm not kidding. When I ran out of that cotton field, got on top of the bag of cotton on the trailer, and sat up there crying, I knew then that I was really going to do something better with my life. I didn't know exactly what that was, but I knew three things. One, I was getting off that plantation. Two, I was going to college. And three, I was going to college to be a nurse just like my Aunt Charmin and Ms. Smith.

So, I had to first start with college. I already knew college was going to cost a lot of money, and my parents weren't going to be able to help me. They were still doing everything they could to take care of my sister and I understood that. That meant that all the financial responsibility would fall on me; I'd have to find a way to raise the money.

I needed a job, and something better than the four dollars I was being paid every Saturday to work at the plantation house. During my last semester in high school, I began by looking through the ads in the newspaper that my grandfather brought home from the plantation house every night. I wasn't sure what I was looking for, but after a few days, I found it. The headline of the ad said, Wanted: Live-in maids in New York.

I got excited just reading that and by the time I read the rest of the ad, I knew this was for me. The agency would pay my way to New York and then send bus tickets if my application was accepted. By the time I finished reading the ad, I was ready to pack my bags and go.

When I sent the letter off so that I could be considered, I prayed that I would get the job. Not only would being a maid give me the money that I needed for college, but I would get away from the plantation at the same time. It would be wonderful to spend the summer in New York.

Just a few days before I graduated from high school, I received a reply from the A1 Agency in Manhattan -- I was accepted!

I cannot tell you how excited I was. And some of my aunts and uncles were excited for me. My Aunt Marie even gave me two pieces of Samsonite luggage for graduation. I started packing; I was ready to go.

My grandmother, though, couldn't believe that I was going to make that trip to New York and stay up there for the whole summer. It wasn't going to be my first time in New York; I'd gone before with my grandmother and one of my aunts from Winston-Salem. I was in the eleventh grade at the time, and my aunt, who often went to Brooklyn to visit her sister, took my grandmother and me along for the ride.

But this was going to be totally different. I wouldn't be traveling with my family, I wouldn't be staying with family. I was going and staying all by myself.

"You really gonna go to New York?" my grandmother asked me.

"Yes, Ma'am."

She shook her head and gave a little laugh. "That's all right, Gal. Someone's gonna hit you in your head and you'll be back here."

I wasn't sure if my grandmother meant what she said or if she was making a joke. Her words bothered me a little, and scared me a whole lot.

But it wasn't enough to stop me. All I had to do was think about picking cotton. And since I wasn't going to do that, I was going to be on that bus to New York.

My parents were a bit more supportive than my grandmother, though no one was jumping up and down ready to see me leave. It was more than missing me. My parents would definitely miss me, but I wasn't the first one to leave home. My brother, Wence and my sister, Rosie had both left the plantation and were living in New Jersey. The only difference between my older siblings and me, though, was that they were living with relatives in New Jersey. I would be going to New York by myself. So of course, that was a concern.

But being on my own didn't bother me. On that Tuesday, two weeks after I graduated from high school, my father took me to the Greyhound bus station in Winston Salem to catch the bus for New York. On the hour drive to the bus station, I wondered if my father was going to give me any advice about New York. But as always, he was a man of few words, and he just hummed along the way. I guess that meant that he was happy with what I was doing. I guess he knew that I would be all right.

So at the age of seventeen, just a few months after I graduated from high school, my luggage and I were on that bus for the sixteen-hour trip from Winston-Salem to New York City. Most of the trip was overnight, so I slept, and then, the next morning we were in New York -- at the Port Authority in Manhattan. I'd been told that the A1 agency was close enough so that I could walk. But one thing I hadn't planned on; I never thought about carrying the two suitcases across Eighth Avenue, which was a huge street that I didn't expect. It was only a couple of blocks, but I struggled. And it took me longer than it should have to get to the agency.

But, I finally arrived. I dragged my luggage into the agency and then left it by the door as I went to register with the receptionist. As I gave her my name, I looked around the huge room. There were dozens of chairs all around, I guess for the girls who were coming for the jobs. And then, there were about six desks all around the perimeter.

"Okay, just sit over there and someone will be right with you."

I pushed my luggage to the corner, then sat as she told me. But it wasn't long before one of the interviewers called my name. She didn't ask me very many questions; I guess it was because I'd answered just about everything on the application. After she reviewed everything with me, she said, "Just go over there and have a seat. You won't be here long; you'll be one of the first picked."

"Really?" I said. "They're going to pick me? I've never done this before."

"Oh, don't worry. They're going to like you. They always pick the yellow girls first," she said.

I was a little shocked that she would just come out and say that to me. But I didn't say anything else and just sat there and waited. There were about a dozen other girls all sitting around on metal chairs and less than an hour later, all of these white men started coming in.

They all did the same thing as they walked into the office -- they glanced at us, then walked up to the receptionist. Then, they glanced at us again. And just like the agent had said, I was picked first.

"Ever Lee," the lady called my name. I jumped

up and went over to the desk. "This is Mr. Erlick," she said.

"Hello," I said as I turned to him.

"So, I'll take you home with me to meet my wife and children," the little Jewish man said.

"Should I take my luggage?" I asked the agent.

She shook her head. "No, you can leave your bags here. You'll just go out there and he'll bring you back. If you like the job, when you come back, you'll fill out the papers and then you'll go back with your bags."

His car was parked not too far from the curb, and I slid into the front seat. On the ride to Brooklyn, he was pretty quiet, which was fine with me because I didn't have anything to say. Plus, it gave me a chance to look out the window and take in the city.

There were lots of tall buildings in Manhattan, but Brooklyn was different. It seemed to be primarily residential, though it still wasn't anything like what I was used to in North Carolina.

When we arrived at the house in Brooklyn, I met Ms. Erlick and their three children. All she did was smile at me, while Mr. Erlick did all the talking. Everyone else was quiet as we walked through the house and he told me all of my responsibilities. It seemed simple enough -- I'd have to do the basic cleaning and cooking and take care of the children, all things that I'd done at the plantation house. And for the summer, I would be paid $35.00 each week, plus lodging as had been advertised in the newspaper.

That was fine with me, so much more than I was earning on the plantation. I was ready to get to work and told Mr. Erlick that I wanted the job.

On the ride back to Manhattan, Mr. Erlick was a bit more talkative than he was when we were going out to Brooklyn. "Your days off will be on Thursdays and every other Sunday," he said. And then, he placed his hand on my thigh. "But, you'll spend those days with me."

I looked down at his hand and froze. I couldn't even look at his face as he kept his hand on my thigh. My grandmother's words and all other kinds of thoughts flashed through my mind.

What should I do? Should I stay in the car? Should I try to jump out? Just thinking about jumping out was too scary for me; I didn't want to get hurt and if I did jump out, I didn't know where I was. How would I get back to the agency?

So, I decided to hold my breath and not say a word as we drove back to Manhattan. When Mr. Erlick parked the car, I jumped out and ran. I ran all the way into the building, up the stairs, and I didn't stop running until I got into the bathroom.

And I didn't even stop there. I ran into one of the stalls, locked the door, and jumped up on the toilet so that no one would see my feet. I was out of breath as I stood on top of that toilet. But it didn't matter. I just stayed there and stayed there. I don't know how long I stayed, but I stayed long enough to be pretty sure that Mr. Erlick had left, and would no longer be looking for me.

When I was sure that he was gone, I tiptoed out of the bathroom and when I didn't see him, I walked over to one of the agents just as she yelled out, "All the girls that didn't get picked today, there's a bus waiting outside. We're taking you to Hempstead and you'll be brought back here tomorrow."

The girls who were left (about six or seven) all started moving out of the room, but I couldn't leave yet. I had to get my bags.

I asked the agent, "Where's my luggage?"

She looked at me. "Where have you been, Ever Lee? We were looking for you."

"I was in the bathroom," I said, not wanting to tell her what happened. I didn't want them to say that they didn't want me.

She said, "We thought you had left, so Mr. Erlick chose another girl. But don't worry; there'll be others coming tomorrow. Now, you'll have to get on the bus."

"But what about my luggage?" I asked her again.

She pointed toward the door. "It's on the bus, just get on the bus."

And so, I did exactly what she told me to do. I jumped on that bus along with the other girls and took the hour ride out to Hempstead, Long Island. We were taken into this big building, kind of like a factory where there were cots lined up for us. We were each given a sandwich and a can of soda and then went off to bed.

The next morning, there were showers where

we were able to bathe, then we got dressed, and ate, before we got back on the bus for the ride back to the agency. Just like the agent had said, there were more men there and just like the day before, I was chosen early.

This time, I was chosen by a couple and right away, I felt better because the wife was there, too. Most of the men came to the agency without their wives and after what happened yesterday, I wasn't sure what I was going to do if that happened again today. But they both seemed very kind when they introduced themselves to me.

"Hi, Ever Lee, we're Mr. and Mrs. Bronstein," the man said.

"Yes," his wife said. "It's nice to meet you."

"Nice to meet you, too," I said.

Then, the man started explaining that they wanted someone to help them for the summer. "We live in Oceanside; that's out on Long Island."

"We have two children, a son and a daughter. But what we mostly want you to do is to help take care of our little girl, Sharon," she said.

He said, "Yes, Sharon has a Kidney disease. She's very sick."

Wow, this is great, I thought. Not that their little girl was sick, but I was used to taking care of my sister, so I knew what to do. I'd be able to help with their daughter.

It felt like this was a sign -- my sister was sick, their little girl was sick. I wanted to go to college to be a nurse, and I was sure that this work would help me get more experience. It was going to help me in my career. So, I went home with the Bronsteins.

Living with them was like living in a mansion. I had my own bedroom, my own bathroom; I had privacy. It was such an upgrade from the way I'd been raised and the way I'd been living.

This was my first step toward my dream -- of never returning to the plantation. And I enjoyed every minute of it.

# Chapter 6

All my life, I'd kept a secret.

Maybe it wasn't so much a secret, maybe it was more like no one in my family wanted to talk about it, so no one ever did. But the secret was that I had a hard time seeing.

I knew that my sister, Rosie, had the same challenges that I had, but we both just did what we had to do to get by. I learned as a young child to compensate for my lack of sight. I learned very early to memorize where I was and where things were in the house and around the house. And when I had to go outside at night to get water, I felt my way around.

Compensating and memorizing were fine when I was in familiar places. But, it was always scary for me to try something new at night when I was someplace I didn't know well.

Like when I was the queen in high school. It was such an exciting time, but I remember wondering if I would be able to see as I walked down the aisle in the auditorium. I'd worried about that for days and it turned out all right because I did have some light perception. I could always follow the light...if there was light.

But if there wasn't light, or if I didn't know where I was, that could be trouble. And because of that, I ran into trouble when I was with the Bronsteins that summer.

For most of the summer, it was fine. I loved being in New York and working, but being there also gave me the chance to get together with my cousin, Erline who lived in Brooklyn. I met Erline when I'd come with my grandmother to New York and so when I was there for the summer, I would go to Brooklyn when I had some time off and we would hang out together. But I always made sure that I got back to Oceanside before dark.

One time, though, I didn't time it right and by the time I pulled up in front of the Bronstein's home, it was already dark. I got out of the taxi and there was nothing but total blackness around me. I couldn't see a thing.

All I could do was start walking and feeling my way to the house. I walked slowly, trying to remember the width of the walkway, trying to remember where the bushes were, trying to remember how many steps I had to take to the front door.

I was sure I was almost to the door when I heard, "Ever Lee?"

I froze.

Mrs. Bronstein said, "Are you all right?"

I couldn't see them, but I knew they were standing there, both of them, watching me. "Yes," I said, "I'm fine." I wanted them to go back into the house and not watch me stumbling. But, I knew they would stay right where they were. All I could do was keep moving. Using my foot, I tried to feel my way.

Now, I was scared for two reasons -- I was afraid of the dark, and I was scared that the Bronsteins would find out my secret since they were standing right there watching me.

It took me a few more moments, but finally, I reached the door. There was light behind the door; there, I could see.

But the Bronsteins stood there, looking at me with frowns on their faces. "Are you all right?" Mrs. Bronstein asked again.

I nodded, but could hardly looked at them.

My heart was just pounding, pounding. They had to know that something was wrong; why was I stumbling to their front door?

Then, Mr. Bronstein asked, "Are you drunk?"

I didn't expect to do it, but I burst into tears. That question made me even more ashamed than I already was. Of course, I wasn't drunk, but for me the problem I was having with my eyesight was something to be ashamed of. I think the shame came because this was something that I'd never discussed. No one told me if this was normal or not. It was never mentioned, so that meant that there was something wrong with it, right?

And if no one mentioned it to me, I never mentioned it either. I just kept all of my fear about my condition inside.

But when Mr. Bronstein asked me if I was drunk, now I had to talk about it. Now, I had to tell the truth. So as I cried, I told them everything. I told them how I couldn't see in the dark, how I couldn't see at all at night. I told them that this was my secret. That I didn't tell anyone and I didn't want them to know because I was afraid that if they knew that I couldn't see well, they wouldn't hire me.

"But, I'll understand if you fire me," I sniffed. "The only thing that I want is for you to send me back to North Carolina. Because I want to go to school. I want to be a nurse."

I was waiting for the Bronsteins to look at me with disgust and tell me that I had to leave. But that's not what happened.

Mrs. Bronstein sat down next to me, took my hand and told me that they understood. "I think you're very brave, Ever Lee and we would never want to fire you."

Those were not the words I expected, but I was so grateful that she said that.

"We want you to stay with us, Ever Lee. You're doing such a good job with Sharon and we want you here for the whole summer."

I was so happy that night. I felt accepted by the Bronsteins. I felt like maybe there wasn't anything wrong with me.

But while I felt good that night, soon sadness came over the entire Bronstein family. Sharon passed away right before the summer was over. She was only five years old. I felt so bad for the Bronsteins, but they were still kind to me. Even telling me that I'd done such a good job, they wanted me to come back the next summer to take care of their son.

Not only that, when it was time for me to leave, they bought my ticket to go back to North Carolina. But it wasn't a bus ticket, nor a train ticket -- the Bronsteins bought me an airline ticket. And, they gave me enough money for my first year in nursing school.

I was so grateful. And now, I was on my way!

# Chapter 7

It was my very first time on a plane.

The flight was just a bit under two hours, and it was exciting to me. But I wasn't focused on the ride as much as I was thinking about what was coming next for me. I was really going to nursing school!

North Carolina Central University, the all-black college in Durham, North Carolina, had been my first college of choice, but there were two reasons why I couldn't go there: I didn't have enough money attend school there, and North Carolina Central didn't have a nursing program. So, I was going to take the exam to get into the Duke University Practical Nursing School.

My Aunt Charmin told me all about the program. "It's really good, Ever Lee," she said to me. "You'll be a practical nurse when you graduate."

That was fine with me; it was my only option, so I was going to make it work.

My Uncle De met me at the Raleigh/Durham airport. I arrived back in North Carolina the day before the exam to get into Duke.

"So, how was the flight?" my uncle asked me as he carried my suitcases to his car.

"It was exciting."

He laughed. "This is an exciting time for you. First New York, now nursing school. You're doing big things, Ever Lee."

He was right about that. I was ready for Duke University. The moment I graduated in June, my aunt had sent in all the paperwork and there were only a couple of things left to do. I was so excited. Nursing School was the first step toward the new life I wanted to have. This was the key that would open up so many doors for me.

I could hardly sleep at my aunt and uncle's house that night; and I got up with the sun the next morning.

"You're sure ready to do this, aren't you, Ever Lee?" my aunt said to me with a smile.

"Yes, ma'am."

My aunt and uncle were amused, but I knew they were proud of me. Even though I had only stayed with them for that one year when I was in the fifth grade, they still believed that I had a lot of potential. And, I was going to do everything that I could to live up to that.

My aunt drove me to the nursing school where the finals tests were being administered and I was ready. But when it got to the eye exam part of the test, I was really nervous. I didn't know what they were going to have me do. And I was afraid, that my secret was going to be discovered. Of course, I failed the eye exam right then. And there went my dream to be a nurse.

When I came out of the test and told my aunt that I'd failed, she couldn't believe it.

"Is something wrong with your eyes, Ever Lee?" she asked me.

I didn't quite know how to answer her. Like I said, I thought my whole family knew; I just thought they didn't want to talk about it. So, I said, "I don't know. I just know that sometimes, I can't see."

"Well, get in the car; we're going to find out."

I wasn't sure what she meant by that, but I slipped into the car and stayed quiet until my aunt pulled into the parking lot of a medical building. "I'm taking you to see an optometrist," she said. "He'll be able to figure this out."

I was scared and excited at the same time. Would this doctor understand what was going on with me? Would he be able to help me and fix my eyes?

When we got into the office, I sat in the waiting area as my aunt stepped up to the receptionist and put our name on the list to be seen. Even when she sat down next to me to wait, I didn't say anything to her. And, I was glad when she didn't ask me too many questions because I didn't know what to say to her.

We didn't wait very long before I was called in by the doctor's office and then, I was given an eye exam where I had to read the letters from a chart.

"Well, young lady," he said after he finished the exam. "I think we can help you."

I held my breath. Would all of the problems I was having with my eyes be over now? Would I be able to see in the dark?

"You need glasses!" he said as if he had just solved all of my problems.

Glasses, I thought to myself. I wasn't a

doctor, but I knew glasses weren't going to help. How could they? When there was total darkness around me, glasses were going to do absolutely nothing, except magnify the darkness.

Of course, I didn't tell the doctor that, and I didn't say that to my aunt. I just took the pair of glasses, knowing that whatever was wrong with me was still there. Nothing was going to change. But now, a doctor had examined me and my aunt would expect me to be fine.

When I walked out of the doctor's office that day, I knew that I was going to have to fight harder to keep up because of my eye problems, and fight harder than ever before to keep it a secret. But I would do whatever I had to do; I would handle it myself.

Even though I couldn't see, even though the doctor didn't know what was wrong with me, and even though I'd just failed the entry exam to Duke University Practical Nursing School, none of that mattered. Nothing was going to stop me. I was going to do something; all I had to do was figure out where and how.

When I got back to my aunt and uncle's house, I started thinking about what I could do, and I focused on my first college choice again -- North Carolina Central.

North Carolina Central was expensive and I couldn't figure out how I was going to pay all of the room and board.

"Well if you go to Central, you can stay with us," my Aunt Charmin said.

I couldn't thank my aunt and uncle enough. That was going to take a big financial load off. But even with that, and with the savings and the gift from the Bronsteins, I was still $31 short, which was a lot of money at that time.

I was determined to make this happen, so I turned to the only person I thought could and would help me. I turned to my grandfather.

Like I said before, I got my love for learning from my grandfather and I knew he was proud of my achievements and my desire to go to college. I knew my grandparents, just like my parents didn't have much money. But, I knew that if there was any way for my grandfather to help me, he would.

So, I called him up, explained to him what happened with Duke University and told him that my only option was North Caroline Central.

"But now, I don't have enough money," I told him.

"How much do you need?"

I took a breath before I said, "Thirty-one dollars."

He was quiet, but just for a moment. "I'll send it to you."

That's all he said. Like I mentioned before, he didn't have very much money and my grandfather sending that money to me meant that he was going to sacrifice something. It meant so much to me that my grandfather believed in me that much.

So, he sent me the money and I enrolled at North Carolina Central. Of course, without a nursing program, I had to choose another major. After a little bit of thought, I chose Business Education. Why? I don't know. All these years, I'd wanted to be a nurse, and I didn't have a backup plan. So when I had to choose a major, I thought about some of the things that I was good at. In high school, I'd done well with typing and shorthand. And, I figured that I could go into teaching. That's how I decided on Business Education.

If I'd had anyone to help me, to guide me, to direct me, I may have chosen something else. But, I had no one; I was seventeen and making these decisions pretty much on my own.

But it seemed like I was doing okay. I had the money I needed, I'd chosen my major, and now, I was going to be a freshman at North Carolina Central University.

The year was 1960.

# Chapter 8

I was in college, but boy was I not prepared.

Just like when I'd gone to the fifth grade in Durham and discovered that the school I'd attended wasn't as good as the city schools, I discovered the same thing again as a freshman at North Carolina Central.

The education that I received at my high school in Davie County didn't prepare me to compete with the students who came from schools in Durham, Winston-Salem, Greensboro and some of the other cities in North Carolina. I even had to take remedial math before I could take freshman math -- which wasn't surprising to me. My math teacher in high school wasn't even a math major at college. My high school just had to use the teachers they had for whatever they could.

But I was determined. I was going to work as hard as I could. Sometimes that wasn't enough though, because of my eyesight.

I tried to get involved in school activities, primarily track because I'd always been a good runner. I really enjoyed it, but my involvement with the team didn't last long after a couple of evening practices. It was impossible for me to jump hurdles in the dark. I was banging up my legs so bad, if I continued, I might not have been able to walk. It just wasn't working. So I gave that up and that was the end of my athletic involvement.

Sometimes my classes were just as bad. While my classes were all during the day, there were a few exams that were given in the evening. The first time that happened to me was with my final exam in Biology. When I walked into that lecture hall, I knew I was in trouble. The lighting was poor and as I took my seat, I tried to figure out what I was going to do.

As the exams were passed out, I prayed that there was enough light for me to see, but when I received my paper, it was just like I thought. There wasn't enough light for me to see the questions. I didn't have a choice; I had to speak to the instructor.

As students all around me were taking the

exam, I walked to the front of the room. Just like all the other times when I had to speak to someone about my eyesight, my heart was pounding.

I wasn't sure what I should say to the teacher, so I just told her the truth. "Professor, I'm sorry, but I can't see this." I held out the paper.

She looked up at me with a frown. As if she didn't have any idea what I was talking about. "What do you mean you can't see the paper?"

"I can't see it," I repeated. That was as much as I was going to tell her, but clearly, it wasn't enough.

She stared at me for a long moment and as she looked at me, it was almost like she was laughing. She had a half-smile as if she was amused. As if she was thinking that this was a good excuse; she'd never heard this one before.

"Just go back to your seat and do what you can," she said in a condescending tone that let me know she thought I was just trying to get out of the exam.

Standing there, I was devastated. She thought I was lying and what I needed to do was tell her the truth, the whole truth. But, I couldn't. I didn't want anyone to know because what if they found out and kicked me out of school? So I did the only thing I could do...I turned around and walked right out of that room.

It was nothing but pride, though at the time, I would've said that I was protecting myself and my secret. Getting my college degree was my goal, it was the most important thing to me. And so that's why I was willing to struggle through it, no matter what the cost.

Of course, I failed Biology, which made me so sad. I'd never failed any classes before. I hadn't even come close to failing.

But even with my challenges on campus and in the classroom, I was determined to succeed. The library was where I spent most of my time. I liked to study, I wanted to study because I knew I had to put in extra effort to make up for my condition. I had to excel whenever I could.

But the problem with the library, though, was that I would stay there for hours, not leaving until it was dark. And that meant I had to struggle to find my way home. My aunt and uncle already lived a good mile and a half away from the school. But add that to the fact that I couldn't see, that was the longest, slowest walk. I had to wait for passing cars to shine their headlights so that I had enough light to see what was in front of me so that I could keep moving.

It truly was a challenging life. I was glad to be in college because I was preparing for my future. But there was a lot of sadness at the same time because I felt like I couldn't be honest. I could never make friends, I couldn't get close to anyone because of the fear that someone would discover my secret.

So although I was where I really wanted to be, and although there were thousands of students on campus, college became a very lonely place for me.

And then, about two months before the end of my first year, tragedy came to my family.

It was my aunt who brought me the news one night while I was sitting at the kitchen table working on my assignments.

"Ever," she began as she sat down at the table with me, "Rebecca is in a coma. She's at Baptist Hospital."

I stayed quiet for a few moments taking in my aunt's words. "I want to go see her," I said, finally. Even though I was used to this -- Rebecca being in and out of the hospital -- something about my aunt's words made this time feel different. I needed to see my sister.

"Okay," my aunt said, nodding. "We'll take you."

We drove over to Winston-Salem. I was going to miss classes that day, but I didn't care. The drive was only an hour, but it felt much long and by the time I got to the hospital, I was really scared. Was my sister going to be all right?

We were met with silence when we stepped into Rebecca's hospital room and I walked slowly toward her bed. I had to step past a machine that made a constant beeping sound in order to get to her. Rebecca was lying there, so still, with her eyes closed. I could hardly tell if she was breathing.

"Rebecca," I whispered as I leaned over the bed rail. I spoke softly so that I wouldn't startle her. "It's me, Ever Lee."

She didn't move.

"Wake up," I told her, speaking just a little louder.

There was nothing. She still didn't move, she

didn't open her eyes.

"Come on, Rebecca. We came all this way to see you." This time, I put my hand on her arm and shook her just a little bit.

"Ever," my aunt came over and stood beside me. "She can't hear you."

"What?" I asked, frowning, looking down at my sister. I heard what my aunt said, but what she said didn't make sense to me.

"She's in a coma. Remember? I told you."

Yes, my aunt had told me that, but I didn't know what a coma was.

"So, she's not going to answer me?" I asked. My voice started to tremble as I realized that my sister was sicker than I thought. Probably sicker than she'd ever been. My aunt shook her head. "No, she's unconscious."

"Well, they need to wake her up," I told my aunt with my voice rising.

"They can't," she said softly.

If they couldn't wake her up, that meant that she was really, really sick. Was she dying? I could hardly breathe as that thought went through my head. This was my sister, the one closest to me. All our lives, I knew how sick she was, but the thought that she was unconscious and that I could lose her was unbearable to me.

I couldn't even begin to think that Rebecca was this sick. "Rebecca!" But this time, I screamed. I just kept screaming her name over and over again. "Please, wake up!" I cried.

Finally, my uncle put his hand on my shoulder. "Calm down, Ever Lee."

"No! She has to wake up."

My uncle who took my hand and led me out of the room. The whole time, he tried to console me. "She's going to be okay, Ever Lee. Stop crying. She's going to be okay."

Outside of her hospital room, other relatives tried to tell me that Rebecca was going to be all right. But, I didn't believe them. I prayed that everyone was right, but I just wasn't sure.

A few weeks later, about a month before the end of the semester, Rebecca died. She never got the chance to go home, she never left the hospital.

Even before we received the call that day that Rebecca was gone, I knew something was horribly wrong. I didn't know it was Rebecca, but I was having one of those days. One of those days when nothing went right.

It started in my classes. I had Physical Ed that morning and we were doing somersaults. Now, I'd done somersaults thousands of times, I was pretty agile and very flexible. But for some reason, that morning, I couldn't do it.

"What's wrong, Ever Lee?" the teacher asked me.

"I don't know. Every time I start to do it, my neck hurts."

He frowned. "Well, sit it out for today," he told me.

For the rest of the day in school, I just didn't feel right. It felt like the whole day was off-balance, so I decided not to stay on campus after classes. I didn't go to the library the way I normally did. I just went back to my aunt and uncle's place.

And my uncle met me before I even got to the door. When he stood there, at the opened door, I slowed down.

"Come on in, Ever Lee." He gestured toward the sofa. "Have a seat."

I was already shaking when he sat next to me. I was glad when he got straight to the point.

"Rebecca died today."

My tears were instant.

He said, "She's better off."

I couldn't believe he said that to me. At that moment, I was so mad at him for saying those words. "I need to get home."

"Okay." My uncle nodded. "We'll be leaving in the morning."

I shook my head. "I can't wait. I want to go now." I didn't wait to hear his answer. I ran to my room and packed my bag. In less than an hour I was ready and told my aunt and uncle that I would just take the bus to Lexington.

"Are you sure you just don't want to wait 'til the morning?" my aunt asked me.

"No, I can't. I have to get home."

I guess my aunt and uncle understood and they drove me to the Greyhound bus station.

I got home that night and there was nothing but sadness when I arrived at the plantation. My parents were there and my other siblings, so that was very comforting. But even though Rebecca had been sick her whole life, and even though this was to be expected, it was still so hard. I just could not believe that my sister was gone.

Rebecca's body was brought to the house in her casket, and that's where she stayed for two days before her funeral. That's how it was then. Families kept their loved ones in their homes so friends and neighbors could come by. The house was full all the time -- with my father's siblings, who came from everywhere to be with us. And then, everyone from church, so many people from the town. All around us, people came with their condolences.

On that following Sunday, we had Rebecca's funeral at our family church, Buncombe Baptist Church. And even though later that day we buried my sister, it was still so hard for me to understand. How could she be gone? She was only sixteen; it just wasn't fair.

My heart was so hurt that I couldn't even think about going to back to school. I couldn't face sitting in those classrooms when my sister was dead.

So for the next month, I stayed home, in the comfort of what was familiar to me. I never went back to school that semester, even though I knew I would end up getting a few Incompletes. I would just make it up at another time.

Right then, I had to stay with my family until it was time for me to go back to New York.

I'm not sure that I was really ready to leave to go to New York. But I had to; it was the only way that I could earn money for my tuition.

So, I headed to New York for the second summer in a row.

# Chapter 9

It was my second summer in New York, and I returned to work for the Bronsteins. I had stayed in touch with them through my first year in college and I returned to take care of their son for the summer. I was really glad to be in New York and not in North Carolina. If I had stayed down there, it would've been too close to Rebecca. And, I knew that I would have to find a way to live with what had happened to my sister.

But I ended up only staying with the Bronsteins for a few weeks. Since I was now a Business Education major, I wanted to do something in my field of study. It just made sense since I'd done well in shorthand and typing and I figured I could just look for an office job that would give me experience and would pay well, too.

A friend of my aunt and uncle's, Vivian, lived in New York, in the Bronx and she told me that I could stay with her. So, after being with the Bronsteins for only a few weeks, I moved in with

Vivian and then started applying for jobs that I found in the newspaper. It didn't take me long to find something and I was hired as a clerk/typist in Brooklyn.

While I loved the job, getting back and forth to work from Brooklyn to the Bronx was always an adventure -- and I'm not saying that in a good way. The best way to travel in New York City is the subway, but of course, it was always darker underground and my vision was getting worse each year.

It was particularly difficult to go from the sun to the darkness of the subway and I just never knew where I was going. But like the way I'd compensated for not being able to see as a child, I did the same thing in New York.

I would get underground and pretend that something was in my eye. Then, I'd turn to the person nearest me.

"Something's in my eye...can you tell me which train is going to Brooklyn?"

I would have to do the same thing when I went from the subway back outside because it would take a few minutes for my eyes to adjust so that I could see. Sometimes I would just walk, feel my way through and move with the crowd. Other times, I would stand off to the side, do that pretend-something's-in-my-eye trick and wait for my eyes to focus. Looking back it was all terribly dangerous.

It was always scary taking that train ride to and from work, but there was one day in particular that was so scary, it almost made me want to leave New York for good. Going home one night, I got on the wrong train and ended up in Harlem. When I came up to the street, it wasn't totally dark, so I could see. But this was one time when seeing didn't help because I had no idea where I was. I was just so scared and didn't know who to ask or where to go.

All around me there were homeless people lying on the ground, men staggering like they were drunk, and women on the streets who looked like prostitutes. I didn't feel like it was safe to talk to anyone.

"Oh, my god," I whispered to myself. I didn't know what to do, but I didn't want to just stand around. I began walking, looking for a place, maybe a store where I could go in and find someone who could help me.

"Hey, pretty lady!"

It took me a moment to realize that the man who'd just said that was talking to me. I took a quick glance at him, and with his long curly hair and polyester suit, I knew exactly what he was -- a pimp!

"See that dress? See that dress right here?" he asked me.

I didn't turn to see what he was talking about and I didn't say a word to him. But that didn't stop him from talking to me.

"See that dress? That would look real nice on you."

I started walking faster, but he kept right up with me.

"I'm gonna buy you that dress and then you can work for me."

Oh, god! I screamed in my head. I don't think there had ever been a time in my life when I'd been this scared. I was walking, but I was trembling. And I heard my grandmother's voice in my mind, "You go to New York and somebody's gonna hit you in your head...."

I was walking so fast, I was almost running and finally, I ran into a small store, a boutique.

"Help!" I screamed. "Please help me!"

A small, older white lady rushed to the front of the store and pulled me into her arms. "What's wrong?"

"Some man is following me," I cried.

"Oh, honey. It's not safe out there. Here, come back here with me."

I didn't know this woman and didn't know where I was, but being in this store with her felt a lot safer than being out there on the street. So, I followed her to the back of the store and she told me to sit down on a stool, while she went further in the back of the store and came back with a glass of water.

"Thank you," I said to her, grateful for more than the water.

She nodded and then said, "You're not from around here, I can tell."

"No, Ma'am," I said before I took a sip of water. I felt calmer as I explained, "I got lost. I was trying to take the train home to the Bronx, but I ended up here."

"Well," she said, "I'm gonna call a taxi for you. They'll come to the back door, so you won't have to go out there." She pointed to the front of the store. "The taxi will take you where you want to go."

I took another sip of water to give me a little time to figure that out in my mind. A cab all the way to the Bronx was going to cost a lot, probably too much for me. "How much do you think that will be?" I asked her.

She shook her head. "Don't you worry about that. I'm going to take care of it for you."

I couldn't believe that she would do that for me. I didn't know her, she didn't know me, but that night, she was like my angel. She did everything she said: she called the cab, and then when the driver came to the back of the store, she made sure that I got inside and she gave the driver the money.

"Thank you," I said to her. "Thank you so much." All she did was smile, sent me on my way and I never saw that lady again.

While that was a scary night for me, it was also an enlightening time. Because as scary as it was, it was such a good experience. You see, I'd grown up in a black world on that plantation, and my experience was that white people didn't treat black people right. From the time I became old enough to understand the real relationship between my parents, my grandparents and the Hairstons, I realized that the white Hairstons never treated my grandparents and my parents fairly.

My grandparents worked on that plantation for their entire life, yet they had nothing. They had never been paid a fair wage for their work, so there was never a chance for them to save money, to get ahead. It took every penny they earned just to survive while the plantation owners thrived because of my grandparents and my parents' labor.

But New York was giving me different lessons. I was learning that everyone black wasn't good, and everyone white wasn't bad. There were good and bad people of every color, every race. Those were the new lessons I was learning everyday -- in New York, in the North. And, I loved the lessons.

Not too long after that, though, it was time for me to return to school. For my second year at North Carolina Central University. The only problem was, I didn't want to go back.

# Chapter 10

It wasn't that I was giving up on college, but I just wasn't ready to go back to my classes. I was still mourning the loss of my sister and not enough time had passed for me to get myself together mentally.

I decided that I would stay out of school. At least for a semester. This would give me the time I needed to get ready and to become motivated again.

But of course, even though I wasn't enrolled in college, I had to do something. I was back in Durham and I couldn't just sit in my aunt and uncle's house all day. Not that I wanted to do that. I wanted to be productive and I wanted to earn money for my tuition when I did decide to go back to North Carolina Central.

So, I applied for a job at S&W, a cafeteria-style restaurant and was hired as a server. I worked the three to eleven shift and my responsibilities as a server were to help the customers after they went through the food line. They'd pick out a table where they would sit, and I'd carry their trays to their tables. It was an enjoyable job because I loved working with people, and it was a pretty good place to work. The customers were friendly, my boss was fair. The only challenges of course, were with my eyesight.

The one good thing about this cafeteria was that it was well-lit. The lights were so bright it always felt like daytime inside, even though it was dark outside during most of my shift. I was able to follow the customers to their tables with their trays with no problem.

The challenge came when the customer wanted dessert or coffee or tea. Because if I was standing across the room and someone was trying to get my attention, many times, I couldn't see them. And it wasn't because of the light. My vision was starting to be impaired at all times, not just in the darkness.

But like always, I found a way to make that work. I'd stay as close as I could to my customers, keeping them all in the same vicinity. So, no one knew about the challenges I had.

S&W was my life during the week and on the weekends, I was with my aunt and uncle, and their daughter, Alma, who was about eight years younger than me. We did the usual family things of a family in the South -- especially on Sundays. First, we went to church and then afterwards, my Aunt Charmin would go to work at Duke University Hospital. We would all ride together, and then once we dropped her off, my uncle, my cousin, and I would often walk around the grounds of the university. Duke is known for its diverse and beautiful landscape that's comprised of quads, open lawns, athletic fields, gardens and plazas. We would walk around, inhaling the fragrances of the flowers, admiring the new plants and lush greenery. It was a gorgeous, peaceful place.

My Uncle De would take my cousin and I home where we spent quiet Sunday afternoons until my uncle went back to the hospital to pick up my aunt late on Sunday night.

The only time I ventured from this schedule was when I went onto campus and attended Sunday chapel. Dr. Ralph Abernathy was a frequent speaker and I really enjoyed the sermons. Not only were they motivating, but they were so informative.

Being out of school gave me more time with my family, but also time to spend with the neighbors that I'd met and whom I now considered friends.

My aunt and uncle lived in a great neighborhood in Durham, filled with families and friendly neighbors who took a liking to me. There were two people in particular who I spent a lot of time with -- Ms. Ford and Ms. Waters.

Ms. Ford lived right across the street. She was married, but didn't have any children, and she pretty much kept to herself. She never sat out with any of the other women, gossiping about things that were going on in the neighborhood. But for some reason, she struck up a friendship with me. She was older, about thirty-five, and I felt like I could talk to her. Many evenings after classes, I would just go and spend time, talking to her about college, and my classes. She was always so warm and open.

I don't know why I connected with Ms. Ford, but I could talk to her better than I could talk to anyone. Even my own parents. Ms. Ford was the first adult I ever really connected to. And she was the first person that I came close to telling my secret.

I never came out and told her directly, but I would give her hints. After I would stay at her house for hours talking, I would tell her, "I can't stay too late. I have to get back across the street because if it's dark, it's hard for me to see." Or, I would say something like, "Unless the street lights are on in the house across the street, I can't see."

No matter how I put it, though, Ms. Ford never said anything in response. All she would do was hug me and the discussion would never go any further.

But even though nothing was ever resolved, it just felt good to be able to get those words outside of me. And with her hugs, I always felt like Ms. Ford was supporting me.

As supportive as Ms. Ford was, Mrs. Waters was encouraging and motivating, too. Ms. Waters lived next door to my aunt and I often went by her house to do little chores for her.

Mrs. Waters was in a wheelchair. She became paralyzed when she was giving birth to one of her children, but not being able to walk didn't stop her from doing what she had to do.

To me, Mrs. Waters was amazing. She could take care of herself. The way she had her home, especially her kitchen organized. She was such a great cook. As I helped with chores around the house, like dusting, changing the linen on her bed, light cleaning, she and I would talk. And she had the most positive attitude. She was a great example for me as I was finding myself becoming more challenged with my eyesight.

Between the time I spent at work, at church, and being with my family and my friends, I began to feel stronger, like I was ready for school. The time off had been good for me, to think, to breathe and to once again become motivated.

So, when the second semester rolled around, I was right back on campus as a full-time student at North Carolina Central.

*** 

It felt good to be back. I was glad to be back in my classes, and I was looking forward to being challenged once again and really getting back into my studies.

A few weeks after the semester began, I met a professor who helped to change my experience at North Carolina Central. He was the head of the Commerce Department, which was where I spent most of my time because of my major.

I first met Dr. Furner when he was my shorthand instructor. I don't know what it was about me, but right away, Dr. Furner took a liking to me. He would call me into his office to do little jobs for him, like picking up supplies, or taking shorthand if he had something to dictate or if he were in a meeting.

I'd spent hours working with Dr. Furner in his office and soon our talks moved from just schoolwork to him asking me questions about myself. Things like, 'what did I want to do' and 'where did I want to go'. It didn't take us long to bond and I loved my relationship with Dr. Furner because it was strictly platonic. I never felt in any way that he was coming onto me or wanted anything more. He wanted to be my friend and in my life, that's what I needed the most.

"I see such potential in you, Ever Lee," he

would tell me. "I really want you to excel."

He believed in me more than I believed in myself. I wanted to believe in myself, but I guess it was hard for me to do that. Especially when I carried around so much shame about my eyesight.

But Dr. Furner gave me confidence and every day, our friendship became stronger.

On the nights when we worked late in his office, he would give me a ride home, which always made me grateful to not have to maneuver home in the dark on my own. After a few trips to my house, I thought it would be good if he met my aunt and uncle.

"I'd like you to meet them," I said one night when he dropped me off.

"Of course, Ever Lee," he said. "That would be lovely."

I was thrilled because I knew Aunt Charmin and Uncle De would be so impressed to meet a professor from the college.

Dr. Furner and I walked to the front door together and I hoped that he didn't think it was odd when I rang the doorbell. Even though I'd been living there for months, my aunt and uncle never gave me a key to their home. I never asked for one, I never asked them why I didn't have one; I just accepted that I didn't and rang the bell every time.

My aunt opened the door, and my uncle was in the living room when we stepped inside.

"This is my professor," I told them. "Dr. Furner, this is my aunt and uncle."

"You're one of the professors at the college?" my uncle asked as he shook his hand. I could tell that my uncle could hardly believe that a professor would actually come to his home.

Dr. Furner nodded. "Yes. I was just giving Ever Lee a ride and wanted to come in and say hello. I know you're proud of her; she's a good student."

"Oh yes, we are." My aunt and uncle beamed. They had always been proud of me, I knew that. But now that Dr. Furner had stopped by, I knew they would be proud and impressed.

"It's such an honor to meet you," my uncle said before he thanked Dr. Furner for taking me under his wing.

Dr. Furner didn't stay very long, though he didn't have to. The good impression was already made. He stayed just long enough to tell my aunt and uncle that he would look out for me on campus and if they ever had any questions, they could call him.

After that, I spent even more time with Dr. Furner. It was just a comfortable friendship and he became my mentor and my confidant.

I began to feel so close to him, so comfortable with him, that I knew that I could tell him the truth. I knew that if I could tell him about my eyes, I could trust him to not embarrass me, or make me feel any more shame about what I was hiding.

So, on one of the nights when we had worked late in his office and he was driving me home, I spoke to Dr. Furner.

"You know, there's something that I've only told once before." He was looking straight ahead as he drove and I was glad because I didn't want him to look directly at me. "Sometimes, I can't see."

He frowned. "What do you mean?"

"Sometimes, I can't see," I repeated. "Especially at night."

"You can't see at all?"

I shook my head. "Hardly at all."

And then, I went on to tell him the whole story. How it started when I was a little girl and how I couldn't see in dark places or at night. I even told him how I was able to get around, and how it had affected me with the track team and even my classes. And, I told him my greatest concern -- that it was beginning to get worse because I was struggling sometimes during the day, too.

"And you've never seen anyone about this?"

"My aunt took me to an eye doctor, but all he did was give me glasses. I knew that wasn't going to help."

"What did your aunt and uncle say?"

I shrugged. "Nothing. I didn't say anything after we went to see the doctor. I didn't want her to know that the glasses wouldn't help. They don't know that I can't see."

He was silent for a while and I knew him well enough then to know that wasn't a bad thing; he was thinking. After awhile, he told me that he wanted me to go see one of the advisors. "I think he can help you. I'll make the appointment."

It felt like a little bit of the weight had been

lifted off of me. Just by telling Dr. Turner, I didn't feel so alone. Especially since he believed me. And, he wanted to do something about it. For the first time, I felt like I was really going to get help.

Dr. Turner set up the appointment for the next day, which was just another reason to give me hope. He believed in me so much that he wanted to help me right away.

But when I went to the advisor's office, I knew almost immediately that this wasn't going to work. It was the way he looked at me when I told him that I couldn't see.

I guess it was because my eyes were opened and my eyes looked normal. To this day, people say to me that I don't look blind and that must've been what the counselor was thinking, because right away, he sounded like he doubted what I was telling him.

"Have you been to see a doctor?" he asked me.

"Yes, my aunt took me to an optometrist."

"So, did he give you glasses?"

"Yes."

"Do you wear them?"

I'd just told this man that I couldn't see anything at night. So how were glasses going to help? But, I didn't say that; I just answered his question. "No, I don't wear them because the glasses don't help. At night, I'm in total darkness and so the glasses don't help anything. That's why I'm struggling, especially in my classes."

"Well, why don't you try the glasses?" he said.

For a moment, I sat there, just so disappointed. And then, I did what I always did. I told him, "Okay," got up and walked out of the office.

That was the end of that.

I ended up feeling sorry that I'd told Dr. Furner. Not that he'd done anything wrong, he was only trying to help. But the counselor made me feel like I shouldn't have said anything. Why was it that no one believed me? That question was what made me feel so bad, and made me feel ashamed. That was why I preferred to hide what was going on with me. It was just safer that way.

So even though Dr. Furner tried to help me, this incident sent me right back into my shell. Dr. Furner never asked me about it and I never mentioned it to him again. But of course, it didn't go away: there was a problem with my eyesight, I couldn't get anyone to help me and I didn't know what to do. So, I did what I always did...I went right back into my shell and kept my focus on keeping up with my studies.

# Chapter 11

Just like the last few years before, I returned to New York for that summer. And, just like the year before, I stayed in the Bronx with Vivian and worked in Brooklyn. Nothing in particular stands out for me during that summer. Maybe that's because that summer was overshadowed by all the events that happened when I returned to North Carolina Central to begin my third year of college.

This was the 60's and we were in the heat and the heart of the Civil Rights Movement. All kinds of speakers came to campus talking to us, rallying us to become a part of the movement.

One of the first speakers to come to our campus was Reverend Dr. Martin Luther King, Jr. Of course, we'd all heard of Dr. King. He was doing big things in the Civil Rights Movement, including the Montgomery Bus Boycott in 1955. We'd been listening to tapes of his speeches and so hearing that he was coming to our college was a major attraction.

Dr. Moore, the president of the college held an assembly to make the announcement and the packed auditorium erupted with cheers. Dr. Moore had to wait for the students to quiet down before he continued with the reason why Dr. King was coming to our campus.

"Dr. King is coming to speak to you about some things that are going on in this city," Dr. Moore said. "He's going to be talking to you about discrimination and integration. He's going to be holding rallies and students from North Carolina AT&T will be joining us.

"Now, it's important for you to know that as a college, we will not be responsible for you. If you choose to participate, my advice is that you contact your parents. They need to know if you want to be a part of the protests with Dr. King."

As soon as Dr. Moore said that, I knew that I wouldn't be calling anyone. Certainly, not my parents. Back at the plantation, they played it safe, they had to if they wanted to keep their jobs. And it wasn't just about their jobs. They knew that it wasn't safe to be part of the Civil Rights Movement. White people were not happy about what Negros were trying to do and they were firing Negros at the first sign that they were involved in the equality movement.

But there were far more dangerous things happening than just being fired. Protestors were being beaten, men were being murdered for being part of the movement.

So I knew without even calling, what my parents would say. I couldn't even tell my aunt and uncle. Even though they were far from the plantation, they were still in the South. They still had white bosses. And even they were afraid of Dr. King and what the movement would do.

That meant that if I was going to be a part of this, I would have to do it in secret. The day Dr. King came to North Carolina Central, the air was electric with excitement. The rally was held in a large open area near the administration building and when Dr. King (and his entourage that included Jessie Jackson) hit that stage, we all cheered.

From the moment he opened his mouth, Dr. King spoke with such passion. "You have to be proud of who you are," he said. "You have to be proud of being Negro."

Then, he spoke to us about integration and our rights as young black people to have equal rights. "You have just as much of a right to work at Sears & Roebuck as anyone else. You have the right to sit at the lunch counter at Woolworth's and be served, just like anyone else. You have the right to watch movies in the theatre from wherever you want to sit. You shouldn't have to only sit in the balcony. You're getting an education, you're contributing to America, and you should have all of these rights."

All of the discrimination that Dr. King was talking about was going on right in Durham. Right where we were being educated, we couldn't be hired. Right where we were being educated, we couldn't sit down next to a white person in many places.

Dr. King was so right to be doing what he was doing and I was impressed. Very impressed with how he talked, how he walked, how he carried himself. He was a proud man who believed in what he was saying and he motivated all of us to believe too!

"We're going to fight for equal rights," he said. "It's going to be a battle, but it's going to be a non-violent war."

He explained that he was going to organize sit-ins and demonstrations and protest marches and he was going to train us to participate in a way where we would get our message across without any kind of violence.

Every time Dr. King spoke, we cheered. His words filled me with such hope for the future. He was such an inspiration; he inspired me to get involved.

After that, Dr. King and his people stayed on campus for several weeks, going back and forth between North Carolina Central and North Carolina AT&T.

Of course, I was still taking a full load of classes, but the preparation for the demonstrations became as important as my classes to me. I decided that I would only participate in the major demonstrations so that I could still keep my focus on my studies.

Most of our preparation was in the form of role-playing. We would sit, and Dr. King's people would call us names, pretend to spit on us, intimidate us in any way they could. And, we learned to sit there, not moving, not hitting back, no matter what anyone did or said to us. We were taught not to react at all.

Those were some tough times, hard lessons, but it was all part of Dr. King's movement. He was going to make a difference through non-violent measures no matter what the opposition did to him.

And soon, we were ready for the protest. Just two weeks after Dr. King first came to campus, we had the first major march. We were over two thousand strong when we marched from our campus to the Sears & Roebuck store where they hadn't hired any black people. The entire time we marched, we kept smiles on our faces, just as we'd been taught. And we kept those smiles, even as white people stood on the sidewalks as we passed by, throwing eggs, rocks, and all kinds of debris. Shouting and calling us all kinds of names.

But we kept on marching. And we kept on smiling. And we kept on singing, something else that we'd been taught to do.

"We shall overcome...."

We kept singing, even when we got to Sears. We sat down on the sidewalks, shoulder-to-shoulder, kept our smiles, and continued to sing.

"We shall overcome, someday...."

It didn't take long for the police to arrive. They were ready for us; of course, they knew all about our march ahead of time. There were no surprises...that was the way Dr. King operated.

The police jumped out of their vans with their batons in their hands.

"Y'all get up on out of here," the policemen, all white men, of course, said in their southern drawls.

Of course, we'd been prepared for this, too. And we did as we'd been taught. We stayed steadfast in our places, still smiling, still singing, though now, we were singing a different song.

"Over my head, I hear music in the air....there must be a God somewhere."

While we were singing and while the police were threatening us to get up and get out of there, Dr. King stood and talked to us.

"Keep doing what you're doing. This is right. We're marching for our rights."

Then, as we were sitting there, we heard the engines of what we thought at first, were cars. But as the roaring engines got closer, we knew they weren't cars. Buses were roaring toward us.

"Oh, my god!" some of the students yelled out.

"Are they going to stop?"

"They're going to run us over!"

But even though we were shouting and screaming, the thing was...we didn't move. Because that's what we were taught...not to move.

The buses stopped right on the edge of where the group began and then, the police came into the crowds and told us to stand once again. When we didn't move, they picked us up, one by one, and tossed us into the police buses.

When one bus was full, that bus would take off, hauling everyone to jail. And then, the next bus would follow. They took us to the jail in downtown Durham, but there were too many of us to book. So, they just packed us like sardines into the cells. And we stayed like that for the rest of the night.

\*\*\*

Dr. King and his people had prepared us for everything -- including getting arrested, but I guess I had never really thought that part through. I didn't know what I would say if I was thrown into jail. And, I guess I didn't think about what would happen if I was kept in jail overnight.

I knew my aunt and uncle would be looking for me. Or would they? There were times I had a feeling that they knew what I was doing with Dr. King. But since they didn't really want to know, they didn't say anything.

Still all night, I worried, that they would be worried about me.

The next morning when we were all released, we had to walk back to our homes. It was quite a walk for me. I had to get back to campus, and then it was still at least a mile and a half to my aunt and uncle's home. It took me a about an hour to get all the way home; thank God it was morning and light outside since I was just so tired.

When I got to my aunt and uncle's house, I went to the back door, thinking that I would be able to get in the house that way since I still didn't have a key. But when the back door was locked, I decided to just walk in through the front.

I knocked and waited. It didn't take long for my aunt to answer the door.

"Where have you been, Ever Lee?" she asked without even saying hello. I could tell by her tone that she'd been worried.

I wanted to just tell her, but instead, tears started falling from my eyes. I think I cried because of all the stress and pressure I'd felt over night in the jail. But, I also cried because I knew once my aunt found out where I'd been, she would ship me right back to the plantation. She wouldn't have a choice.

"I was in jail...."

She gasped.

"Because I was marching with Dr. King." I was sure by then that our demonstration and all the arrests had been on the news.

The look on my aunt's face was a mixture of disappointment, fear, and anger. She opened the door wider so that I could step inside, but she didn't say another word. I was glad that my uncle had already left for his job at the American Tobacco Company. I wouldn't have been able to face him, too, right then. I would need the day to recover, and by that night, I'd be able to tell him what I'd done.

But the thing was, my uncle never mentioned it. And it was days later when I realized that my aunt had probably not told him. She was probably so scared that she didn't want to discuss what I'd done at all. My uncle's job was one where he probably would've been fired if his boss had heard about me. So, my aunt decided not to say anything to my uncle or me.

I didn't have anymore overnight visits to the jail because that was the main march with Dr. King and the only one I participated in. He did many more of course, but because I was working hard to keep up with my classes, I only did that one.

That one was enough because school, and the pressure of my eyesight getting worse was keeping me busy. I had to study harder and longer because now as I read, my eyes would tear heavily.

Then, there was the added social pressure of people wondering why I didn't want to hang out, and why at my age, I didn't drive. Of course, I didn't even have a driver's license, though I did get my driver's permit when I was in high school.

But I didn't go any further than that. I couldn't.

I just kept working hard, doing everything that I could to hide my condition. And that meant I couldn't even date. There were guys who were interested in me, guys who wanted to take me out. But I always made up one excuse or another. Dating was impossible. How would I be able to keep it a secret if I were out with someone at night? As we walked, I would be stumbling for sure. No, dating was much too dangerous.

But then, my aunt and uncle set me up. They had friends at church who had a son, Robert, and both my aunt and uncle and his parents thought it would be good for us to go out together.

Robert was also a student at North Carolina and so he came over to my aunt and uncle's house to see me a couple of times. He was a nice enough guy and we spent time talking about all kinds of things: our classes and music since I loved to sing. We talked about church and things happening on campus.

I felt comfortable enough with Robert so that when he said, "Ever Lee, I want to take you to the homecoming dance," I thought that was a great idea.

It was my third year at NCCU, so I was excited to go. My only concern was that the dance was, of course, at night and that always worried me. But, since I'd spent so much time with Robert, I felt that I would be safe with him.

And the night of the dance, everything was going so well. We met up with a few friends in the gym and we sipped on punch and ate the food that they had there for us.

After we'd been there for about an hour, Robert told me, "Ever Lee, I'm going over there. I see a couple of guys I know." He pointed to the other side of the gym.

"Okay," I said, feeling completely relaxed.

As Robert walked away, I started talking to one of the guys I'd seen around campus. We were just chatting and laughing a little. Nothing was going on. I didn't know this guy that well and I was just waiting for Robert to come back.

After just a few minutes, I saw Robert marching toward me. "I need to speak to you, Ever Lee," he said. The way he snapped at me, I could tell he was angry. I wondered what had happened when he went to talk to his friends.

What had they done to him?

"Okay." I hardly had a chance to say goodbye to the guy I'd been talking to. Robert grabbed my arm and pulled me outside.

"What's wrong?" I asked him when we were alone.

He didn't say a word a first. Just lifted his hand and slapped me so hard that not only did he leave my face stinging, but he left a welt on my neck. "Don't you ever disrespect me like that again!"

I had no idea what he was talking about and that's what I told him as I held my hand to my face.

"I was motioning for you to come over to me and you just stood there talking to that guy. You were disrespecting me!"

"I didn't see you," I cried. "I couldn't see you."

But all Robert did was growl and tell me again to never disrespect him.

He didn't have to worry about that. The good guy that my aunt and uncle wanted me to go out with turned out to be a long way from good. I couldn't believe that he'd hit me like that. But what I couldn't believe more was the reason why. I'd been hit because I couldn't see.

I knew that I shouldn't be going out with anyone. And this proved it.

After that, I didn't date at all. I just did everything I could to do what I had to do to graduate from college.

# Chapter 12

That summer, I was back in New York. Working there was just the best way to earn money for tuition. I was back in the Bronx with Vivian working for a shipping company in the Bronx. It was an administrative position. I was responsible for writing up all the orders and getting them out. It was easy enough for me and I enjoyed that job a lot because it didn't challenge my eyesight. It was clerical duties with a lot of writing, but I felt so comfortable because there were no issues with my vision. I could read my own writing, and the reports were easy enough.

Everything about that summer was easier. Living and working in the Bronx made traveling back and forth a whole lot easier. I was able to catch a bus right in front of where I was living, all the way up to my job. It was a simple commute; when I got off the bus, I only had to walk one block. I could easily do that.

That would've been an uneventful summer if it had not been the summer of '63. Because the summer of '63 was the March on Washington. Although I didn't plan to spend another night in jail, I wasn't going to miss the march, especially when I found out that Dr. King was added as a last minute speaker.

So with four other girls that I knew from school who were working in New York, too, I got on an early morning bus and we took the five-hour trip from New York to Washington. The ride was long, but exciting. Anticipation was building with each passing mile.

At the same time, though, I was just a little anxious. My anxiety came from all the warnings I received from Vivian, and even people that I worked with.

"Be careful down there. The police are going to be there."

"Don't take any money on you, don't take your purses. Leave all of that kind of stuff at home."

"There may be trouble down there."

It was well reported in the news that other groups were going to be at the March, trying to stop us, and trying to start trouble at the same time. We knew to stay together, not to venture away on our own. I was going to follow all of the instructions and listen to all of the warnings. But even with all of that, I was still excited.

Of course, no one in my family knew that I was going. After being arrested, I would never tell my aunt and uncle. And of course, I would never, ever mention this to my parents. Every single one of them would have told me no for sure.

But I didn't feel like I had to tell my parents, my aunt and uncle nor anyone else. I was grown now, living on my own. This was my decision. And as inspired as I'd been by Dr. King before, I was definitely going.

We got to DC a little before noon and the speeches had already started. I was just glad to find out that I hadn't missed Dr. Maya Angelou nor Dr. King. Those were the two I wanted to hear the most.

My friends and I stood with the crowd. It was a mass of people, like a sea of human beings that went as far as the eye could see. We stood together, one on top of the other, everyone packed together, everyone peaceful and just happy to be there.

What was most amazing to me was that the crowd wasn't anything like I expected. The way the news had it, the way the march had been promoted, everyone thought the crowd was going to be all black.

But there were people of every color, of every age. And not just from the United States. People came from all over the world.

And we all loved it! You could almost reach out and touch the excitement.

People were shouting and cheering for every speaker. We heard Julian Bond and Wyatt Walker. And then, there was Dr. King.

He inspired us with his first words, talking about how he was there to cash a check for life, liberty and the pursuit of happiness. But then, Mahalia Jackson yelled out, "Tell them about the dream, Martin. Tell them about the dream."

That was when Dr. Martin Luther King took the speech up to a level where every single person in that crowd was touched. To this day, I still get chills every time I even think about his words.

The march was over before dark, which was a good thing and we were able to get back to

New York that night. On the entire ride home, I played over every moment of the day, hearing the speeches in my mind. It had been such a wonderful day, an amazing experience that I really needed at that time.

That summer had been such a lonely time for me. I was depressed. Even though I knew people, I didn't spend much time with anyone because my eyesight was getting worse. I was trying to figure out what I was going to do, and I just had no idea.

The March on Washington was pretty much the extent of my social life that summer. I didn't even go to spend time with my cousin because she lived too far away. So, my life consisted of working, going home, and some evenings, I would go across the street to a Dunkin Donuts store. That may not sound like much of an adventure, but I loved to go there because of the juke box that I could play. And no matter when I went into that store I would play something -- most of the time it would be Nina Simone.

While I made that trip as often as I could, it was quite a challenge to even get to the donut place. I had to cross a major street and all I had to guide me were the street lights. My focus the entire time was not to trip and fall.

Somehow, I always made it. And, for hours it would just be me and my music. It was that music that got me through my third summer in New York. And music prepared me for my final year in college.

# Chapter 13

My fourth year was going to be my longest year in college because I had to make up for the time I lost when my sister passed away. Even though I had only missed a month of school that semester, I had to make up the entire semester because I missed final exams. And then, of course, I had stayed out the entire next semester. So, I had a lot of catching up, and a lot of work to do.

Even though the Civil Rights Movement was still going on, it wasn't as prominent because so many things were happening in Washington. After the March on Washington, legislation was being enacted to enforce integration and a change in the laws. So much was happening that there just wasn't as much activity on the campuses anymore.

But no matter what was going on in Washington or on the campus, I stayed focused. My mind was filled with thoughts about my classes and my future. As I was coming to an end of my college career, what was I going to do?

That was one of my questions. I was also trying to figure out where was I going to work? And the big question -- how was I going to manage with my poor vision?

Even my aunt was beginning to notice that something was wrong with me. I was sitting at the kitchen table one night, reading and trying to work when my aunt came in.

My aunt stood over me for a moment, but I didn't look up. I was studying. Then, she interrupted me.

"Ever?" she said my name softly. "Are you crying?"

That was when I looked up at her. A couple of tears streamed down my cheeks as I said, "No, it's just that my eyes are very watery."

"Why?"

"I don't know. This happens when I read."

"Well, we can't let that happen," she said. "I'll take you back to the optometrist. You need stronger glasses."

I didn't bother to tell my aunt that glasses wouldn't help. The pair I'd been given before didn't do anything. But still, a few days later, I let her take me back to the eye doctor. And of course, all he did was give me glasses -- that I would never be able to use.

I just had to work harder. And that's what I did. I did the best that I could.

I made it through the first semester, and then in the second semester, I had an internship on campus that Dr. Turner had gotten for me. I worked in the Athletic Department as a stenographer, giving me even more practice in my major.

That second semester was tough for me, though. Because that was when I was supposed to graduate. Of course, I knew this time was coming, but it was tough to handle as the students that I'd started with at NCCU were all preparing for their graduation, and talking about their upcoming jobs.

But I kept my head down and just worked hard, even working through that summer. For the first time, I didn't go to New York. I took a class at summer school -- Biology. I finally made up for not taking that final exam in my first year.

With just one class, I went back to working at

S&W and then, when the summer ended, I enrolled for my final semester at NCCU. From September to December, I took all the rest of classes that I needed to finally complete my courses for my degree. To be honest, there is not much that I remember from my last year in college. I think I blocked a good deal of that semester from my mind because that was such a sad time. I felt like a fish out of water, like I didn't fit in anywhere -- I had missed the graduation march the previous May with my class. And, I didn't want to march with the class of '65. I had made up my mind not to do it.

But even before I had finished out my final semester, I was feeling the pressure to march with the class of '65 and I didn't want to do it. My Aunt Charmin and Uncle DeEdward were the two who wanted me to march the most. They believed that I had worked so hard, they believed that I needed to march and receive my degree.

When I finished my classes in December, I did stay in Durham. I went back to work at S&W and began to make plans. But by February, I'd made up my mind to leave Durham.

This wasn't a quick decision. For the entire

year, I'd been putting a lot of thought into my future. Just like how I knew I had to leave the plantation when I graduated from high school, I knew I had to leave the State of North Carolina, now that I was a college graduate. There just weren't going to be a lot of opportunities for me in North Carolina, especially if I wanted to teach. That's what I decided that I wanted to do.

The idea to become a teacher wasn't mine alone. Dr. Turner had been encouraging me in this direction for a while.

"I think you oughta teach, Ever Lee. You would make a great teacher."

Like always, his confidence gave me confidence and I wanted to become a teacher. I didn't have my teaching certificate, but I had a degree. So, I knew that I could do it. And, I was going to do it in New Jersey.

My brother, Wence, my sister, Rosie, and many other relatives were in New Jersey. Wence had gotten married a few years before, and he told me to come live with him and his wife.

So, in February of 1965, I made my move. My brother drove down from New Jersey, packed me up, and I headed up North. I officially left the state of North Carolina with dreams to become a teacher. And, I was going to do everything I could to accomplish that goal.

# Chapter 14

New Jersey was nothing like Durham, North Carolina.

I felt free and frightened at the same time. Free because I was a college graduate and I was ready to do great things. But at the same time, I knew that seeking employment would mean that I had to face a whole new set of challenges.

But, I welcomed the change. I was happy to be near New York.

I moved in with my brother and sister-in-law on Wildwood Avenue and went right to work, looking for a job. I went through the newspapers every day, and when I wasn't searching for a job, I was spending time with my family.

That was one of the things I loved about being in Camden; I was close to so many of my relatives who had migrated to the North from the South. Between my brother and my sister and their families and my aunts, and uncles and cousins, there were always so many people to see. My time was filled with my family and going to church. There was never a moment of feeling lonely. Life was great for me.

My sister, Rosie, only lived about six or seven blocks from where I was staying with Wence. So almost every day, while I was still job-hunting, I would just walk over to her house and visit with her.

One day, though, I didn't go to Rosie's house just to visit. I went with a specific purpose. Now as you know, my sister had had very bad eyesight her whole life, much worse than mine. So, I wanted to go over there and help her a little. I wanted to help her clean her house.

When I got there, I put on one of her husband's old white shirts, tied up my head, and went to work. I'd been dusting, and scrubbing, and cleaning for a couple of hours when her husband and one of his friends came into the house.

There I was, in that old shirt, looking pretty raggedy by this point. I had to look a mess.

But that didn't stop my sister's husband. He and his friend walked right up to me.

"Sherlock, I want you to meet my sister-in-law, Ever Lee, " Bernard said. He started bragging on me. "She just got out of college, and now she's looking for a job. We know she's gonna get one of those big-time jobs," he said proudly.

My brother-in-law may have been impressed with me, but I knew I didn't look at all impressive standing there, probably covered in dust.

"Well, nice to meet you, Ever Lee," Sherlock said, looking me up and down. Then, with a grin, he added, "You don't look much like a college graduate."

He and my brother-in-law laughed and I had to laugh with them. I mean, what else was I going to do? I knew I was a mess, and they were just teasing me.

After Sherlock and Bernard joked for a few more minutes, they left and I didn't think anything more about Sherlock. I just went right back to cleaning.

About a week later, I was in downtown Camden, very excited because I was having my first job interview. I was applying for a management position at the Bank of New Jersey. The ad in the classified section of the newspaper listed the job description, and with my college degree, I knew I was a perfect fit.

So when I walked into the Bank of New Jersey that morning wearing my best suit, and holding my resume in my hand, I was confident and ready.

With my head high, I walked up to the receptionist. "I'm Ever Lee Hairston, and I'm here for the job interview."

The middle-aged white woman gave me a long look before she made a gesture for me to sit in one of the chairs against the wall.

Then, she stood, and rushed into the office behind her. A couple of minutes passed before she came out. "Ms. Hairston, you can come into the office now."

I followed her into the office and greeted the man, then sat down.

"So, you're here to interview for the job?" he asked.

I nodded, and then went into the little speech that I'd planned. "Yes," I told him. "I'm a recent graduate from North Carolina Central University in Durham and I have my Bachelors in Business Education." I went on to tell him a little about my classes, my strengths and my weaknesses and he sat there, very politely, listening to me.

When I finished, I expected him to ask me a few questions, but he didn't. He folded his hands together on the top of his desk and said, "Well, Ever Lee, you speak well, you're dressed very professionally." He paused. "But I just have to tell you, we have never hired any blacks in this bank."

His words froze me. I sat there not able to move. I was shocked, not only from his words, but I was shocked because of the pain of his words. It felt like a knife had pierced my heart.

Wasn't this New Jersey? Wasn't this the North? I expected this kind of discrimination in the South. I knew about all the prejudice down there. That's why I had marched with Dr. King. But to have the same thing here?

This was 1965!

Even though all of those thoughts were in my mind, I just stood up, said, "Thank you," and walked out of the door with my head held high. But as I walked out of there, I was in a daze, thinking did this really just happen?

I walked down the street, still trying to process what that man had just said to me. I went over it in my mind, still wondering if I'd heard what I knew I'd heard. I was so out of it, that a couple of minutes passed before I realized a car was following me. Well, not exactly following...the car had pulled up beside me and was moving slowly along the curb as I walked.

I stopped and then, I frowned at the unmarked police car. What now? After what happened in the bank, I knew anything was possible.

Then, the man spoke from the window. "Hi! You're Rosie's sister, right?"

That was when I recognized him. It was my brother-in-law's friend, Sherlock.

I nodded because the lump in my throat stopped me from speaking.

It must've been the look on my face that made Sherlock ask, "Are you all right?"

I shook my head.

He said, "Get in the car. I know where Bernard is and I can take you to him."

Tears started rolling down my cheeks and I let it all out. The shock had turned into hurt. Here I was a college graduate, I'd earned my degree the old-fashioned way, working so hard for it, and I got turned down for a job because of the color of my skin.

In 1965!

"Come on," Sherlock said. "Get in the car. Get in the back."

I was too upset to do anything else and I slipped into the back seat.

When he slid into the driver's seat, he said, "I'm gonna take you to your sister's house."

Again, all I did was nod.

He let me stay quiet for a few minutes and then he asked me what happened. I told him the whole story and added, "I can't believe it. Here in New Jersey there's prejudice against blacks?"

He chuckled. "Honey, you just got a rude awakening, didn't you?"

When he did that, I kind of relaxed. There was nothing I could do about it, so I might as well get over it and get back to job-hunting.

As he drove, we chatted and I was surprised when he said to me, "I know Rosie has bad eyesight and Bernard told me that it runs in the family." He paused and apparently, looked at me through the rearview mirror. "Are you okay?"

I shut right up. That was my second major

shock of the day. I couldn't believe he was asking me that; I couldn't believe that Bernard had told him that. We never talked about it in our family, but I guess some of us talked about it outside of our family.

I'm sure Sherlock could tell that I was upset by his question. He said, "I only asked because maybe I can be of help to you."

I shook my head. "No, thanks."

I didn't know this man. And, I'd had enough disappointment with people trying to help me. From my aunt and the optometrist, to Dr. Furner sending me to the counselor. Nothing worked. People helping me only made it worse.

I didn't say another word to him until he pulled up in front of 1455 Wildwood Avenue where I lived with my brother. I couldn't get out of the car fast enough. "Thank you," I said, and thanks for not taking me to my sister's house.

By the time he said, "You're welcome," I was almost in the house.

For a couple of days both of those things bothered me -- the banker and Sherlock. Both of them had said things to me that they shouldn't have said.

A few days later, I was just standing on the porch, enjoying the afternoon and seeing what was going on in the neighborhood, when Sherlock's car stopped in front of the house.

"Hey," he called out to me.

I nodded my hello to him.

"I'm Sherlock," he said as if I didn't know.

"I know."

"Come over here for a minute; I want to talk to you."

Reluctantly, I moved from where I was and walked slowly to his car.

When, I got there, he smiled and said, "Look, I know you were upset about what happened the other day at the bank and I know quite a few people in town." He started naming all the people he knew like one of my uncles, and a couple of people who were with the Board of Education. "I think I can help you get a job."

"Really?"

Sherlock told me exactly what to do and because of his contacts, I eventually got a job with Adult Education program with the city of Camden, New Jersey. Because I was new and fresh out of college, I was hired into a federal-funded program that turned out to be such a blessing for me -- I was finally able to get my teaching certificate. Being part of this program, I was sent to Glassboro State Teacher's College for my credentials. At the same time, I was going to be working in a Title II specialized program, working with adults who were on welfare, teaching them, preparing them, getting them job-ready.

Finally, I was doing exactly what I wanted to do and I was happy. Not only did I love my job, but I wasn't that challenged with my eyesight. Maybe it was because I was used to compensating, but I knew what to do to make it through the days. I took a problem like writing on the board and made it easier on myself by writing big, using large print letters.

Maybe I didn't have challenges because of the gift that I have for teaching. Truly, I believe I have a gift to teach and it was that gift that got me through those times when I needed a little extra help. My gift compensated for everything else.

Now, I had my first job as a college graduate. I was on the verge of having a whole new life.

# Chapter 15

1965! What a profound year for me. So much happened. . . I suffered through my first discrimination in the North, I finally got my first job, and then, I began dating Sherlock.

After he helped me get my job, Sherlock came over to my house to visit a couple of times and it didn't take much to see that he was after me. At first, I didn't want to do it, not after my last experience dating. But after Sherlock asked me out a couple of times, I decided that it wouldn't be that bad. I mean, he was a nice guy who genuinely seemed to care about me. And, he did help me get my job.

So when he asked me to go out to dinner with him, I agreed. We went to a beautiful restaurant in Philadelphia, which was only about twenty minutes away from Camden. It was a romantic place, with a waterfall at the entrance, very dim lighting and soft music in the background.

As we sat and talked, I realized that I did enjoy talking to Sherlock. He was very intelligent, charismatic, and caring, and of course, I loved looking at him since he was very handsome.

After the waiter came to pick up our dinner plates, I asked Sherlock, "Do you know where the restroom is?"

He looked at me for a moment before he said, "You know, I'm a gentleman. And, I'm a policeman so I'm very protective. I'm going to walk over with you and show you where it is."

I knew what Sherlock was doing. Because he'd talked to my brother-in-law, Sherlock knew something about my eyesight and I guess he suspected that I would have trouble walking to it. I didn't know what he knew, but Sherlock knew enough. Plus, he was a detective with the Camden Police Department, so he was pretty observant. He probably noticed that I'd had a little trouble when we'd first come in.

So, Sherlock could have said, 'Well, let me take you to the restroom 'cause you're not going to be able to find it on your own.' But he didn't say that. He didn't say anything to make me feel self-conscious and I appreciated that.

We left the restaurant shortly after I came from the restroom, and in the car, we picked up our conversation where we left off.

But after we'd been talking for about ten minutes, Sherlock said, "I'd like to take you to Will's Eye Hospital over in Philly."

His statement came out of the blue to me and I didn't say a word because now I was concerned. How much did he know? What did he know? What didn't he know? All of those questions bothered me because I didn't have a clue.

We were quiet for the rest of the ride, but when he stopped the car in front of my apartment, he said softly, "Ever Lee, I really think you should do this. Just go and see. I'll make the appointment. All right?"

I didn't know why I was so hesitant. Maybe it was because of all that I'd been through before. Or maybe it was because I still carried so much shame.

"Come on, Ever Lee," he encouraged.

I could hear the concern in his voice and finally, I nodded slowly.

So, Sherlock made the appointment and a few days later, he took me to Will's Eye Hospital.

From the moment I walked into the hospital, I knew this was going to be a different experience from all the ones I'd had before.

When the receptionist gave me paperwork to fill out, Sherlock said, "I'm going to go to work, but I'll be back to pick you up and I'll keep checking on you."

Even though I had been reluctant to do this, already I was grateful to Sherlock. Once he left, the examination went into full gear.

"We have a few tests that we want to do," a nurse said to me as she took me into the Retina Department and sat me in a chair. "You just relax and we'll take care of you, okay?"

She was trying to make me comfortable and I was relaxed, but I did have a little anxiety.

The first test consisted of her putting three different drops into my eyes.

After that, the ophthalmologist, Dr. Klein came in to speak to me. He explained all the tests that they were going to do and he asked me if I had any questions.

When I just shook my head, Dr. Klein said,

"We're going to take care of you today, Ever Lee." He patted my hand as if he understood everything that I'd been through.

He was so kind, so patient and he worked with me for the entire day. Of course, he was in and out and the nurses helped me the most. But he kept checking on me, explaining every single thing that they were doing. He explained it all, step-by-step as he studied my retina and looked at the optic nerve.

After hours of being there, I finally, finally, finally had a diagnosis for my eye condition. After all these years when I was told that I was wrong, when I was led to feel that there was nothing wrong with me, and that I was just crazy, I was finally told the truth.

"You have Retinitis Pigmentosa," Dr. Klein told me. And then, he went on to explain that Retinitis Pigmentosa RP is an inherited, degenerative eye disease that causes severe vision impairment and often blindness.

"The progress of RP is not consistent," he continued. "However, your symptoms already include night blindness and tunnel vision. It's a very rare eye condition and right now, there isn't a lot of research being done on it. But it's being diagnosed more and more and I believe over the years, they'll make advances." And then, he was honest with me. "You will probably go blind, Ever Lee," he said softly, but sternly. "It won't be overnight, it will be a slow process, but it will probably happen."

That had to be one of the most emotional moments for me. It was freeing, in a way. I finally knew what was wrong. But then, on the other hand, what the doctor had just told me was devastating. I was going to be blind and that scared me.

I was so glad that Sherlock was there to pick me up because I needed to get home and be by myself for a while. I needed to digest this information. As he walked me to the car, he asked, "Are you all right?"

I nodded because I didn't know what to say. I was full of so many emotions.

But once we got into the car, I couldn't hold back the tears.

"What's wrong?" he asked.

"They gave me a diagnosis." I paused before I told him, "I have Retinitis Pigmatosa."

"What does that mean?"

I was still crying when I told him about my day and everything that Dr. Klein had said to me at the end.

"Well, how much do you see now?" he asked me.

"During the day, I can still see fairly well. The only problems I have during the day is if I'm trying to read, especially for long periods of time. But it's very hard at night or in the dark. If I'm out, I can hardly see at all."

He was quiet for a moment. "Well, we have to keep digging. We're going to find a cure."

"Dr. Klein said there is no cure right now."

"Oh, I don't believe doctors," he said waving his hand in the air like he was dismissing doctors.

I loved that Sherlock didn't want to give up on this, though I knew the truth. I was going to go blind and it made more sense for me to learn to deal with it rather than deny it.

It did help that Sherlock was there with me. He was the first person to whom I'd ever disclosed everything. He knew it all, and he believed me and wanted to help.

When I got home, I took some time to go

over the information that Dr. Klein had given me and digest the information. I was going to go blind. I said that a couple of times trying to get ahold of what I felt about that. And then, I thought about my sister. Since this was nothing that we had ever talked about before, I felt that I had to tell her. At least then, she could go, get tested, and find out for herself.

So, I called my sister and before she answered the phone, I tried to think about all the ways to tell her. When she answered, I just said, "Rosie, I've been diagnosed with having something called RP. I think you should go and have all those tests done so you can find out."

And my sister simply said, "I already did."

It took a moment for her words to make sense to me. She had already done it? And, she didn't tell me? But then, it made sense. She'd gone for the tests, but then she did what we'd always done in our family, she didn't talk about it.

And we didn't talk about it then. I hung up and we didn't say another word.

The only person I could talk to was Sherlock and maybe that was one of the reasons why I started getting closer to him.

# Chapter 16

Sherlock Houston was a safe place for me. Since he already knew everything about my condition, I could date him without any issues. I didn't have to hide, I didn't have to pretend. Sherlock knew me better than anyone in the world at that point. And that was very comforting to me. I felt very connected and secure with him.

We dated and began to build a life together. Sherlock was involved with lots of things. He was an entrepreneur in his heart and one of the businesses we did together was a clothing business. He would go to New York, buy the clothes, then we'd throw home shows, where I was the model. We did pretty well financially with that.

Besides our business venture, we spent lots of time together, visiting with my family, going to church, sightseeing in New York, and hanging out on the boardwalk in Atlantic City. In lots of ways, Sherlock empowered me. He was always so proud of me -- that I was working, that I was living my life, even though he knew there were times when I was struggling.

His confidence in me gave me confidence in myself. Sherlock knew my secret, yet he stayed by my side.

After our first two years together, we began to talk about marriage and that made sense to me. We were close to each other, he knew everything about me. I believed he was the man that I was supposed to spend my life with.

At least, that's what I thought until I found out that he was seeing someone else.

One day, I was in his apartment and I found a compact in the bathroom. Then, in his bedroom, there were clothes that obviously belonged to a woman. I couldn't believe it. I was so very hurt and I told Sherlock that.

"I'm so sorry, Ever Lee," he said when I confronted him.

"I can't believe that you did that to me," I cried. "I thought you cared about me."

"I do. I love you, and what I did had nothing to do with you."

All I could do was shake my head.

"I'm going to end it with her."

I guess I looked at him like I didn't believe him because he said, "Really, I am. I'm going to break it off because you're the one I want to be with."

"No," I said. "It's over."

"No, it's not," he said. "I know you love me. I know it's not over."

But I guess the thing that Sherlock didn't count on was that being with him had given me a lot of confidence. I was working, I was living on my own. So, I decided that if Sherlock didn't want me, then I would go out with a man who did.

At the school where I was working, there were two teachers who were interested in me, but I had never reciprocated because I was dating Sherlock. Unlike Sherlock, I never wanted to cheat on him.

But once I found out about this other woman, I decided that I would date Jim, one of the teachers that I knew.

The only problem was my dating Jim didn't get very far. On the night that we went out to dinner, Jim noticed on our way home, that Sherlock was following us.

"Sherlock is behind us," he said.

"What?"

"Yeah," Jim said. "Sherlock keeps pointing his finger and telling me to pull over."

Jim didn't stop and Sherlock followed us across the bridge from Philly back into Camden. And he didn't stop there -- he followed us all the way to my apartment.

When Jim got out of the car and opened the door for me, Sherlock pulled up right behind us.

Sherlock jumped out of the car. "What are you doing?" he shouted.

I didn't know if he was talking to me or Jim.

But then, Sherlock clarified it when he told Jim, "This is my woman. You need to leave her alone!"

I couldn't believe Sherlock was doing this. A grown man confronting another grown man this way. And why was he doing this? He didn't want me, but he didn't want anyone else to have me?

Jim held up his hands. "Look, man. I don't want any trouble."

That was when I jumped in. "What are you

doing?" I shouted to Sherlock. "Just leave us alone!"

We went back and forth like that for a couple of minutes. I was so embarrassed and I was so angry.

When Sherlock finally left us alone, Jim told me, "Ever Lee, I like you a lot, but I can't handle this. That man's crazy and I don't want to get into anything."

Now, I was angrier than before. Was Sherlock serious? Was he really going to follow me on every one of my dates?

I got that answer quickly because Sherlock did it again. I dated the other guy at my school, Alfonzo. And somehow Sherlock found out about it and did the same thing.

After the second time, I began to think that maybe Sherlock really did love me. Maybe everything he said about it being a mistake and how he really wanted me was the truth.

Looking back, I have very different emotions now, than I did then. It's clear now, that I was in a fog and my listening to Sherlock was based on my emotions rather than intellect. But, I went with my emotions, Sherlock and I got back together, continued dating, and got married in July, 1969.

I was excited and happy to be the first girl to get married at Buncombe Baptist Church. Not only was it newly built, but it was our family church that was located in Pettersville, in Davidson County in North Carolina. It was extra special to me because that was where my mother grew up.

Sherlock and I had a big wedding, with one hundred and fifty guests. Family and friends came from all over to help us celebrate first at the church, and then celebrate at the reception that we held on the plantation.

Then, the next morning, we left for our honeymoon in the Bahamas, a wonderful week away on Paradise Island. But when we got on the plane to come back home to New Jersey, little did I know that my honeymoon was about to be over already.

# Chapter 17

If there is a time that I have to define as one of the most hurting times in my life, it would be right after I got married. Who would have thought that when our plane took off from the beautiful Bahamas, that I was heading toward some kind of hell?

Sherlock and I had just spent seven glorious days in the Bahamas taking in the island, relaxing on the beach, and hanging out in the local restaurants and clubs, and spending time with another couple that we met at the resort who were also honeymooning. I'd had such a wonderful time and though our honeymoon was over, I was looking forward to our life as husband and wife.

When we landed in Philadelphia, Sherlock held my hand as we walked to baggage claim. And then, he gathered our luggage. We'd left our car at the airport, but before we went to the parking lot, Sherlock stopped to make a call. He called Naomi, the woman he'd been seeing, the woman who'd almost broken up our relationship.

"I'm only calling her because I don't have enough money for us to get over the bridge," Sherlock told me.

I felt horrible when she met us and brought the money. I watched the two of them, and it just looked like two friends together. But no matter what I saw, and no matter what he said, I felt in my heart that Sherlock was still seeing Naomi. But he insisted that he wasn't.

"I only love you, Evie," he said. "We just got married, didn't we?"

I was trying hard to believe him, but the truth was I didn't. I just didn't have any proof. Plus, he was right. We had just gotten married. I had to give our marriage a chance.

So, I put my head down and focused on my new husband and my life. I was determined to build a good life for us.

It wasn't hard being with Sherlock. There were so many wonderful things about this man who'd stolen my heart. Besides the obvious that he was very handsome, he was intelligent, a go-getter, and always so charming. But while he had all of those strengths, there were times when those strengths felt like weaknesses to me. Sherlock had big dreams, which was one of the things I loved about him. There was always a new business venture that he wanted to start. But big dreams and new businesses cost money, and after awhile, his new ideas put a strain on our finances. It was a lot of pressure financially.

And then, on top of that, I still had my suspicions about Sherlock and Naomi. But Sherlock always assured me that I was wrong. He wasn't having an affair; he only wanted me.

So, we lived our lives like every newlywed couple, happy, and learning more about each other. In February, 1970, just seven months after we were married, I found out I was pregnant. Sherlock and I were both excited. I'd stopped taking my birth control pills, wanting to get pregnant right away, so this was thrilling to me. Both of us were looking forward to this addition to our family.

Then, I found out that my girlfriend, Renee was pregnant, too. That just made it more exciting for me. Renee and I spent a lot of time together, and she ended up taking me to many of my doctor's appointments while Sherlock worked.

And this was a great time with Sherlock, too. He was attentive, we spent a lot of time together, hanging out with Renee and her husband, having picnics in the park. It was really beautiful for me.

Then, in July, we celebrated our first wedding anniversary with a trip to Niagara Falls. Oh, what a beautiful time that was!

Sherlock came home a few days before our anniversary with a gift for me. I was delighted and when I opened up the package, I gasped at the beautiful black maternity dress he'd purchased for me.

"This is gorgeous, but what's the occasion?" I asked him.

"Pack this with everything else you're gonna need," he said.

"What?"

"We're on our way to the airport. It's our anniversary and we're going away for the weekend to celebrate."

I was so excited and had a ton of questions for him, but Sherlock hardly told me anything.

I found out soon enough when we flew into

Niagara, New York, then we rented a car and drove over to the Canadian side. Those were three amazing days where we toured Niagara Falls, ate at wonderful restaurants, and talked about our future together.

I felt like I was living such a blissful life, but right in the middle of our joy, tragedy struck. My sister, Mary Louise, got pneumonia. She was hospitalized, but they couldn't get her blood pressure down and she died. She was only twenty-two years old.

It was such a shock to all of us, and everyone was particularly concerned about me because I was eight months pregnant. But that wasn't going to stop me from celebrating my sister's life.

Mary Louise was living in New Jersey so we first had a memorial service for her there. And then when she was taken home to North Carolina, I took a flight down for her services. We laid my sister to rest in October, 1970 and Victor was born in November, 1970.

\*\*\*

I was thrilled to have my new son. From the

moment I'd received my diagnosis of having Retinitis Pigmentosa, I knew that I was only going to have one child. I didn't know much about RP, except that it was genetic. So, I was willing to take the risk once, but not more than that.

So Victor was it for me and I felt blessed that he was a healthy baby in all ways.

If life had been like that all the time, I would've had an amazing marriage. But I felt like the first year and a half was an emotional roller coaster for me. Sherlock could be attentive, he could be loving, but I was still always filled with suspicion. It was the way Sherlock behaved. He was the president of the Black Policeman's Organization and we had to participate in many of their functions. I would've had a good time when we went to the fundraisers and other events -- except Sherlock was always flirting...heavily...with other women. I always left those events feeling insecure and so bad.

So, I was up and down. At home, Sherlock was loving, charming and attentive. But then we were out, I felt like he was all over other women. I just knew that he was having an affair. I just didn't have any proof.

But then, the proof came around our son's first birthday.

We had planned a big birthday party for Victor and as we were setting up for the celebration, Sherlock told me that he had to take a trip.

"I have to go away tomorrow," he said. "It's business."

That was odd; why hadn't he told me this before?

"The department is sending me to Mexico."

Okay, Mexico? And he was just telling me? I didn't believe it and I told him that I didn't believe a word he was saying.

"It's true, Evie (the name he and others in NJ were calling me). It's really true," he kept saying over and over again, like he couldn't believe I thought he was lying.

I shook my head.

"I don't know why you don't believe me, honey." He pulled me into his arms and kissed me. "I'm going to miss you so much, but I have to do this for work." Then, he reached for Victor and picked him up. "I'm gonna miss you, too, son."

Now, I knew he was lying. He was trying too hard to convince me. All of a sudden, he was the perfect husband, the perfect father...oh, he was lying for sure.

Our guests arrived for the party and I wore a happy face. But inside, I kept thinking about Sherlock's trip. Even though he greeted and entertained our guests with enthusiasm, and he joked and laughed with everyone, I still knew that he was lying and something was up with this trip to Mexico.

We didn't talk about it again for the rest of that day. Not even when everyone had left. But that night, I watched him pack, filling his luggage with all kinds of summer clothes: shorts, tank tops, sandals.

"I'm really going to miss you, Evie," he said as he folded each item into his suitcase. "Maybe one day we'll take a trip to Mexico."

I didn't call him a liar to his face; I just called him a liar in my head.

The next morning, he kissed me goodbye, hugged Victor, then left. I stood at the door and watched him get into a taxi. Before he got into the car, he turned back toward me and with a huge smile on his face, he waved.

I didn't move. I just watched that taxi drive away.

Then, I sat down in the living room and thought about every word that he'd said to me. If the department was sending him to Mexico, wouldn't this have been a trip that they'd planned for months?

About ten minutes passed before I stood up and grabbed the telephone. I knew the telephone number for the cab company by heart and I dialed.

When the dispatcher answered, I said, "My husband just took a cab and he left something at home that I must give to him. I need to know where the taxi dropped him off."

I gave the dispatcher the details of where he'd been picked up, and she gave me the drop-off address. It wasn't anywhere near the airport...it was at Naomi's apartment.

I was in tears before I even hung up the telephone. Two years. We'd barely been married two years and Sherlock was doing this. It was hard to believe in my head, but in my heart, I'd known the whole time.

There wasn't a lot of money in the house; I tried not to keep money there. But I had enough for what I needed to do. I dressed my son and dropped him off at Tina's, my girlfriend, who lived in the same complex as Sherlock and I did.

"Is everything all right?" Tina asked me.

I didn't want to cry and I knew I would if I talked to her. "I have to check something out. I'll let you know when I get back," I told her.

Then, I called my own cab. And I had them take me to the same address. On the entire ride over, all kinds of thoughts were going through my head. How could Sherlock do this? Why would he do this? Why did he lie? And why did I ever try to believe him?

When the driver stopped in front of her house, I sat in the back of the cab, staring at the building. I didn't have a plan, so what was I going to do when I knocked on that door?

I envisioned the confrontation and shook my head. This wasn't me. I wasn't this type of woman. This was Sherlock's life, not mine.

"Can you take me back, please," I said to the driver.

And without a question, he turned around and took me home.

On the ride back, I made my decision. Sherlock wasn't worth it. My marriage that had barely started was on its way to being over.

*** 

Although I knew what I had to do, it still wasn't easy.

When the cab dropped me off, I went straight to get my son; right now, I really needed him. My plan was to get to Tina's house, pick up Victor, and then just come home.

But when Tina opened the door, I couldn't help it, I burst into tears.

"What's wrong?" she asked me.

I shook my head as I stepped inside. "Sherlock is cheating on me and I think he's been cheating the entire time that we've been married." For the first time, I told Tina everything that had been going on with Sherlock from the time I first caught him with Naomi. I hadn't shared what had happened or my suspicions with anyone before. All my life, I'd hidden parts of my life, I kept secrets. I was used to doing that back then and that's what I'd done now.

But on this day, I told Tina everything about Sherlock and actually, it was very cathartic to get it all out. The secret that I'd been carrying about me and Sherlock was a heavy burden.

When I left Tina's house, she came with me and stayed with me through the day, until that night. Even though my heart ached from the pain of Sherlock's deception, it was comforting to have her there.

But once she was gone, it was just me with my son, and my emotions. I spent a restless night thinking about Sherlock in Mexico with Naomi. Thinking about how he was sure that he'd fooled me. I couldn't wait for morning to come, but when it did, I didn't feel any better. I couldn't eat, I could barely take care of Victor. But thank God he was there because without my son, I may have stayed in the bed all day and just cried.

Of course, Tina called. "I'm just checking up on you," she said.

"Thanks, I'm okay." We both knew that wasn't true.

"Do you want me to come over?"

"No, not today. But come over tomorrow. I have a plan."

All day long, I thought about what I was going to do and the next morning when Tina arrived, I told her. "I'm going to find Sherlock and Naomi. I'm going to call the hotels in Mexico."

"Who are you going to call? There are hundreds of hotels in Mexico."

I shook my head. "I know, but I know he's in Acapulco, so I'll start there. God will direct me with the rest."

That was the first time Tina laughed since I'd told her the news about Sherlock. "Yeah, right."

She may have thought that was funny, but I said what I believed. I knew God was going to give me all the help that I needed and I truly knew in my heart that I was going to find Sherlock. So while Tina sat and watched me, I got to work.

First, I called information and got the names and numbers for a few of the hotels. I didn't say anything to Tina as I made the first call and asked to speak to the guest, Sherlock Houston. I was told that there was no one there by that name. I made the second call and the same thing happened. By then, Tina, shook her head and leaned back on the couch. I could tell that she thought it was going to be a long afternoon.

And then, I made the call to the third hotel.

"Hello, I'm trying to reach one of your guests...Sherlock Houston."

"Just one moment, please," the operator said. "I'll connect you."

When, I said, "Thank you," and looked over at Tina and she sat straight up.

Tina whispered, "You got him?"

I nodded as the phone shook in my hand. I was trembling so hard, I had to take deep breaths to steady myself.

The phone rang three times, and then, I heard, "Hello."

It wasn't Sherlock. It was Naomi.

From the moment I'd taken the cab to her house, I knew they were there together. But now, to hear her voice, to have definitive proof was a lot to take in. I kept my composure, though, even though my heart was beating so hard and so fast my chest was hurting in a way that I'd never felt before. I really was concerned; was I about to have a heart attack?

But if I was, my heart attack was going to have to wait because I had to hear what Sherlock was going to say.

"Hello," Naomi said again.

I said, "Well, I knew that this was true, but I had no way to prove it. Now, I do." I knew she recognized my voice. "Let me talk to Sherlock."

That's all I said to her. I didn't say hello, I didn't greet her in any kind of way except to tell her that I knew she was with my husband.

Once I said that, she didn't say anything else to me, but I could hear movement through the phone, then whispers, and finally, my husband's voice.

"Hello."

"You liar!" I screamed.

"Evie!"

"You cheated, you're just no good. Do you know that you've stripped me of everything?" I cried.

"Evie, calm down."

"How can I be calm? It's over, Sherlock," I said, releasing my pain through my tears. "It's over."

"Evie, you're talking out of your head."

"What?"

"You're not making any sense."

He was in a hotel room with another woman when we'd only been married for two years and we had a son. And now, this man was telling me that I was the one who wasn't making any sense?

"If I'm not making any sense," I said, "then, you get back here today."

"Evie, I can't do that."

"Then, it's over." And I slammed down the phone.

I could hardly move as I held my head in my hands.

Tina came over and sat next to me. "Ever Lee, "I'm so sorry," she whispered as she put her arms around my shoulders.

I sat there sobbing, feeling like I was losing my mind.

"I'm going to call Yvonne," I told Tina, referring to our other friend. And, I did.

When Yvonne arrived, I told her the whole story and like me, she couldn't believe it. By the time I got to the phone call I just made, she said, "Pack some things, you're not going to stay.

You're coming home with me."

I was so grateful for that because now that I knew everything, I didn't want to stay in that townhouse for another minute. This was the place where Sherlock and I had started our life together. This was the place where we were supposed to be planning for our future, raising Victor, and growing old together. We weren't supposed to crash and burn before we even celebrated our third wedding anniversary.

So I did as Yvonne said, packed a bag for me and my son and stayed with her.

Being with Yvonne helped so much. I had someone to talk to and discussing it all with her made me feel a little less crazy. But after a couple of days, I decided to go home. As far as I knew, Sherlock was still in Mexico. I just wanted to be back in my own place and Yvonne understood that.

The only problem was, when I got home, I couldn't stop the thoughts that were going through my head. I was thinking all kinds of things and after being back in the townhouse for just a couple of hours, I felt like I was losing my mind.

As I walked through the rooms that I'd shared with Sherlock, I couldn't stop thinking about all the different ways I could really get back at him. I devised all kinds of plans.

My first plan was grits. I decided that I would boil some grits exactly the way Al Green's girlfriend had done. That story had been in the news so much; everyone had heard about how his girlfriend had thrown hot grits on Al Green while he showered. So, I decided that that's what I would do. When Sherlock came home, and went to sleep, I would throw a whole pot of grits on him. That wouldn't be difficult; Sherlock slept hard. So by the time he figured out what I'd done, it would be too late.

But then, I wondered if the grits would really hurt him? So, I searched for Sherlock's gun. As a detective, he kept two or three in the house and one was always in the closet. Once I found the gun, I decided that shooting him would be better.

But then with my eyesight, what if I missed? So, I went back to the grits. The grits would just have to be enough for my payback.

I was obsessed with those kinds of thoughts; I felt like I was going crazy. Thank God! I could laugh at myself. When I told Yvonne what I'd been thinking, she laughed and said, "Evie, have a drink. You have to do something to relieve all your stress."

That was probably a good idea, except I wasn't much of a drinker. Beyond a glass of wine with dinner, I didn't care for alcohol all that much. Plus, I had to take care of Victor. I wasn't going to drink and not be able to care for my son.

So, drinking was out, since that wasn't going to help me think clearly. And, my mind had to be clear so that I could figure out what I was going to do.

But no matter what I did, my mind wasn't clear. Because that first night back when I returned home from Yvonne's, I discovered that I needed milk. Now, I could have easily called Tina or Yvonne, but with all of these thoughts, I needed to get out of the car.

I still hadn't gotten my license because of my eyesight. But, I'd learned to drive back in high school, and since I'd been with Sherlock, I'd done some driving. He would make me drive during the day, encouraging me to do it, making me feel like I could do anything and that he would always be in my corner.

Well, now I knew that wasn't true.

But, the times he'd made me drive were coming in handy now since I needed to get to the store. It was still light outside, so I figured that I could drive myself. It would be a quick trip and give me a chance to get away from this townhouse for a little while and all the thoughts that were going through my head.

The grocery store was less than a mile away, so I strapped Victor into the car, and jumped into the driver's seat. I got to the store easily enough, went inside, and walked through getting what I needed and a few more things.

But by the time I got back outside, a windstorm had come up. And the sky that had been clear not long before, was now really dark. I got my son and I back into the car, but the moment I turned on the ignition, I knew this was going to be a real problem.

I couldn't see.

What was happening to me? Everything that could go wrong seemed to be going wrong and I sat behind the wheel of that car and thought about how horrible my life was. I'd married a womanizer, a man that I loved and had shared all of my secrets. I gave him my life. And now, here I was in the middle of this storm and no way to get home.

But I had to get home because Victor was with me. He was the reason that I had to go on. I had to take care of my son.

Right behind me, a man turned on the lights to his car and pulled out. Quickly, I did the same, following the lights. Now, I had it figured out. I knew the route that I had to take and I could see the lights. So, all I had to do was follow the taillights that were going in my direction.

When the car I was following turned right, I pulled over and waited until a car came along that made a left. When that happened, I followed those taillights.

The truth is, I don't really know how I made it home that night. But I had to do it. I had my son. And, I had to take care of him.

Actually, I wasn't sure when Sherlock was coming back. And once he came back, I didn't know if he was coming back to our townhouse.

But, I didn't have long to wait. The next

evening, Sherlock came home. I hadn't had any time to prepare since I didn't know when he would arrive. So, I was just sitting in the living room.

When he walked in the door, he paused and we stared at each other for a moment. Then, he put down his bag by the door.

"Hello, Evie."

"Just tell me why."

He hesitated, then said, "I'm too sleepy. I'm too tired to talk."

Then, he walked by me as if that was the end. And I did the only thing that I could do. I was filled with hurt. I was raging with anger. And so, I grabbed him.

I grabbed his penis.

And, I pulled. And, I squeezed.

And Sherlock screamed.

"Evie, let me go. Let me go!" he said over and over, trying to pull away.

But I had a strength that I didn't even know I had. And the more he screamed, the more I twisted. He tried to shove me away, but I had a death grip on him. We tugged back and forth for a while, though he never raised his hands to me.

He just tried to get away. But, he couldn't.

"Evie," he kept shouting.

I still wouldn't let go.

Finally, I must've weakened just a bit. Just enough for Sherlock to pull away. He stumbled backward and you could see that he'd been in a battle. His pants were ripped.

"What is wrong with you?" he was huffing and puffing. And the way his face was twisted, I could tell that he was still in pain.

I didn't say a word to him. I just glared.

I could tell he wanted to me to say something, but he wasn't going to get to close. So, he backed into the bedroom, keeping his eyes on me the whole time. Once he grabbed the telephone, I went back into the living room.

I could hear him talking to my Aunt Emma. "I need you to come over," he said. "Something's wrong with Evie. I think she's lost it."

Lost it? I thought. Was he kidding? There was nothing wrong with me. I knew exactly what I'd done. And if I had the chance, I was going to do it again.

But I didn't have the chance. Because Sherlock didn't get close to me again, and my aunt was there in less than thirty minutes.

She rushed into the door. "Ever Lee, what's wrong?" She was the right person for Sherlock to call. My Aunt Emma was my dad's youngest brother's wife and she was a strong, dynamic woman. "What's going on?" she asked.

Sherlock stood by the bedroom door, shaking his head. But, he stayed far away from me. "She's lost it," he had the audacity to say again.

"I haven't lost it!" I shouted. "This man has mistreated me."

My aunt looked from me to Sherlock. And then, I told her the whole story.

At the end, she said, "Ever Lee, it's going to be all right. Just come and stay with me."

I shook my head. "No, this is my home. He needs to be the one to get out."

I didn't know what my aunt would say to that, but she looked up at Sherlock and said, "Well then, you need to leave. You need to be the one to get out."

Sherlock didn't protest at all. "Just give me a few minutes and I'll get a bag."

Ten minutes later, he was back out the door.

In a way, I was surprised that he'd left. I thought it was going to be much harder. But then, I guess Sherlock thought about what I'd done to him with my bare hands. And, he'd probably heard the story about Al Greens and the grits, too. I'm sure he didn't want to take the chance with one more night with me.

# Chapter 18

The only good thing about this timing was that I'd taken off a year from work when my son was born. And though he'd just turned a year, I was going to have to be going back to work soon.

So I had time to get my things together and get out of that townhouse. It didn't take me long; I didn't want to be there anymore.

I called my brother, told him what was going on and he agreed to help me move. Wence decided to take the furniture that I wanted, and he would store it until I got my own place.

I didn't want much, just the living room set, which Wence took for me. And then, I took my bed and Victor's crib and we moved in with my sister who now lived in Willingboro, one of the suburbs. My plan was for this move to only be temporary. I just needed time to raise enough money so that I could get my own place.

I didn't see Sherlock again for about a week. He didn't come back to the townhouse while I was there, but he came out to Rosie's several times, always saying the same thing.

"Evie, I really want you to come back home. We're married and I love you."

Sherlock was as charming as ever. He had so much charisma and if I hadn't just been through all of this with him, I might have believed him because he sounded sincere. And in an odd way, I believe he meant what he said. He did love me, he did want me back. But he was a womanizer and I believed that he would always be that way. The same way he was charming me, he was charming everybody else and I just wasn't having it anymore.

So it didn't matter to me how many times he called, or how many nice things he said, I was done. I was never going back. I knew what Sherlock Houston was -- and I didn't want that in my life.

It took a little bit of time for Sherlock to really believe me. He asked me to reconcile our marriage right up to our divorce. But he finally got it -- he realized that I wasn't coming home and so we worked out an arrangement for him to still see Victor regularly. That was important to me. I wanted my son to have a relationship with his father, and so Sherlock would pick Victor up, and spend time with him.

But that wasn't the only time I saw Sherlock. We'd developed a routine where he would pick me and Victor up in the morning, we'd drop Victor off at nursery school, and then Sherlock would drive me to work. In the evening, we would repeat the routine.

It may seem crazy, but with my eyesight failing, taking the bus was becoming more difficult and was quite a challenge with Victor. So, Sherlock helped out in that way. I wasn't going back to him, but he continued to try to take care of me.

Very quickly, I got used to my new life. I was back at work, would come home and take care of my son, and spend time with my sister and her family. I stayed with Rosie for five months and I could've stayed longer. But, I really wanted a place of my own for me and my son.

In April, Victor and I moved into a one-bedroom apartment in Maple Shade, New Jersey. I probably could have moved out even sooner, but not only was I saving for an apartment, I was saving money to go on vacation with my family. We all planned to travel to Spain in June, and I so wanted to go on that trip.

It was important to me for so many reasons. I wanted to travel while I could still see, and while Victor was still young. It turned out that I was right. The trip was wonderful because it was a way for me to get away from all that I'd been going through, all that had been happening.

That seven day trip was quite a refresher for me and I came back feeling much better and optimistic about my future. The one-bedroom was a good starter apartment for me and I moved up a bit when I moved up to the second floor into a two-bedroom apartment. Now, Victor had his own room.

That apartment complex was a good place for me to be because Judy, my sister-in-law lived there as well. We'd been married to brothers and Judy was already divorced. But we spent a lot of time together because she had one daughter, Michelle, and I had Victor.

It was because of Judy that Victor and I got out so much. I'd told Judy about my eye condition, but that didn't matter because she had a car. So we did all kinds of things with our children. We went to church and to parks, the kinds of things that I wouldn't have been able to do alone with Victor. Having her in my life was a major asset and that's why till this day, she's still my best friend.

Even though Sherlock and I were separated, we often got together with Victor -- especially when Victor started auditioning for commercial work. An agent in Morristown, New Jersey saw Victor and told me that he thought Victor would be great for commercials. So after getting all the information and having Victor sign with an agency, I would take him into New York for the auditions. Often, it would be just me and Victor. And sometimes, Sherlock would go with us. It would be an all day venture by the time we took the bus from New Jersey into New York, then seeing one casting director after another, moving from trailer to trailer. But I was happy to do it. It gave me something to do with Victor, and it gave me something to focus on because things still were not going well with Sherlock.

By this time, Sherlock and I had been separated for well over a year, though we were still not yet divorced. I didn't have the money to file, and Sherlock was still determined to fight me all the way.

I didn't understand Sherlock's determination to fight me on the divorce, especially since he was now seeing somebody else...besides Naomi. It was just the strangest thing. A few months before, Sherlock had opened up his own detective agency. He'd opened the business with Naomi, but he was dating one of the investigators who was working for him.

And the situation became even stranger when this woman would call me up. Of course, Carol had gotten my number from Sherlock and she would call acting like she was interested in me, and acting all friendly. But I didn't trust her; I knew better. I knew that Sherlock was behind it.

I wasn't sure what he was up to exactly. I knew he'd been telling people that I wasn't allowing him to see Victor, which was a lie. So, I kept my guard up and was on the lookout all the time.

It was a good thing because one day Sherlock and Carol came to my door. When I opened it, I was surprised to see them both standing there.

Usually Sherlock came to get Victor. But this wasn't a scheduled time. And why did he have Carol with him? Another one of his women? Please! My guard went up immediately. I didn't trust him or her.

"What are you doing here?" I asked Sherlock.

Victor had been standing behind me in the apartment and Sherlock and Carol started calling out to him. "Hi, Victor. Come here, Victor."

My son was only four at the time and he was of course, happy to see his dad. So he came running to the door. And when he did, Carol snatched my son's arm. It was only my reflex that made me grab him and try to pull him back.

But she held onto him, and I did, too. And there we were, tussling over this four-year-old.

"Let go of my son," I shouted.

Victor started crying, "Mommy!"

I held onto him until Sherlock and Carol finally let go. And then, they left.

My heart was beating so fast as I closed the door, but I didn't have time to think about what had just happened, what Sherlock was trying to do.

Victor was still crying. "Daddy, Daddy!" he

called out for his father.

"It's okay, sweetheart," I tried to console him. "Daddy!"

"I know, honey," I said, giving him a hug. "He'll be back. He'll be back to see you and to get you, okay? Don't worry."

Still, I wasn't sure what that had been about. Was Sherlock trying to take Victor? Or did he just want him on a day when he wasn't scheduled and he felt that was the best way to get him? I didn't know. But I already didn't trust Sherlock and that situation just made it worse.

The good thing was that Judy was still such a major part of my life and it was so good when Victor and Michelle could spend time together. One of the best activities for the two of them was the pool that was part of the apartment complex.

I just loved it when the two of them could play in the pool together. Judy and I would sit on my balcony and we could look down from the second floor and watch them as they were playing in the kiddy pool.

We did this day after day in the summer and one time, when we were out on the balcony just having one of our regular girl chats, Judy jumped up suddenly.

"Oh, my gosh!" she screamed. "Oh, my gosh!"

I scooted to the edge of my chair. "What?"

"Victor," she yelled, not answering me at all. She dashed out of the apartment, and I was sitting there helpless.

"Victor," I started screaming, too. I couldn't really see what was happening, but I knew for sure that Victor was in trouble. My heart was pounding as I waited and I kept calling for my son.

Finally, Judy called up to me and told me that Victor was okay. I had never been so scared; I'd never been so relieved.

She brought Victor back to the apartment and I hugged him as she told me that Victor had jumped from the diving board.

From that day, I was determined to make sure that my son could swim. Judy and another neighbor taught Victor how to swim.

Life was like that for me and Victor. Always an adventure.

And with it just being the two of us, many

times Victor had to look out for me. Even at a young age, Victor was so helpful to me. Part of it was because I couldn't see, but another part of it was because I was just so scary.

A good example of this was when we were told there a field rat had gotten into our building. Just the thought of a rat made me want to scream, so thinking that one was in our apartment building really had me frightened.

From the time I heard that, I took extra precautions. When we would step out of the apartment and walk to the elevator, I would tell Victor, "Hold Mommy's hand. And look out for the rat, and if you see anything we have to run!"

He'd just say, "Okay, Mommy."

Well, we always made it from our apartment to the elevator, but then, there was the day when I was sure that I'd found the rat -- right inside my apartment.

I'd been gathering clothes for the laundry, and I was inside my walk-in closet. As I was pulling clothes down, I felt like something had jumped from the top shelf down to the floor.

The rat!

I was sure it was the rat, and I'm telling you, I

started screaming and screaming and screaming. I ran out of there, jumped on top of the bed and was still screaming.

Victor came running into my bedroom. "Mom, what is it?"

"Victor! Look, look, look," I said, pointing to the closet. "Go in there and tell me what you see. Tell me what you see!"

I was shaking as I waited for Victor to go in there and investigate. I wouldn't be able to stay in this apartment if the rat was living in here with us.

Just a couple of moments later, my son walked out and very calmly said, "Mom, it's just your wig!"

I jumped down from my bed thinking all of that for nothing. I had to find a way to get over this fear. But I really didn't. Whether we were in the hallway or even down in the laundry room, I had Victor on the lookout.

In the laundry room, I had him standing on top of the machines, checking behind them before I would put clothes in. My son took it all in stride. He would do it just so I wouldn't be afraid.

And if anyone asked him, he'd just say, "My mom is afraid. Very afraid."

Victor was right; I was too afraid to stay in that apartment complex, even though it was very nice.

So, my son and I made our next move. We moved into our townhouse.

# Chapter 19

Moving into the townhouse wasn't the only change in my life. Sherlock and I were finally divorced. He was ordered to pay child support, but it wasn't always easy to get it from him. It was a hassle and a headache because so much was going on in his life.

About a year after our divorce, Sherlock married again. And the shock to me was that he married Naomi.

He didn't come out and tell me that, though. I'd found out because when he wasn't paying child support the way he was supposed to, I called and threatened to take him to court.

A few days after that conversation, a check came in the mail...from Naomi, with a note: This is for your child support.

The kicker was the way the check was signed: Naomi Houston.

I guess that was the way she wanted me to know that she was his wife now. And that was fine with me. She could keep him.

Still, Sherlock was always around me, because of Victor, of course. But dealing with him with our son was another hassle. Sherlock would take Victor on the weekends and wouldn't bring him back. I'd have to call and call, and finally, he'd bring Victor home. Sherlock would show up, when he was supposed to and it just always seemed to be a problem. Really, it was just drama. Anytime I had to deal with Sherlock, it was drama.

And it wasn't the ordinary kind of drama. To someone looking in from the outside, Sherlock was a very good man. He would come over to where I was living and after a snowstorm, he would shovel the snow for me and then all the neighbors. He would make sure that all the driveways were cleared and the walkways were cleaned.

Everyone who saw that would say, "Oh, my gosh! What a perfect man he is. Why would Ever divorce him?"

This wasn't just coming from friends and neighbors. Even my family would ask me why did I divorce such a wonderful man? My mother and father couldn't believe I left him. Especially when they got to see him when they would come up to New Jersey for the holidays. Sherlock would be right there, bringing food, always cheerful, always charming.

With his actions, it was like he was telling everybody, "Here I am, the perfect man, I'm the perfect dad and Evie divorced me. What's wrong with her?"

People asked me those questions all the time and that brought a whole different kind of stress onto me because I chose not to belittle or destroy Sherlock's reputation. I figured that eventually people would find out the truth. They would find out who Sherlock was for themselves.

Everyone was right about one thing, though. Sherlock may not have been the perfect husband, but he was an overall good guy. Even though we were divorced, he did continue to take care of me.

There came a time, though, when I got the chance to take care of Sherlock. I was home when I received a call from Naomi. "Evie," she said.

Just hearing her voice made me want to hang up the telephone, but I didn't.

"Yes," I answered her.

"Evie," she repeated my name again. "Sherlock is in the hospital."

It took a moment for those words to register in my head. "What happened?"

Naomi went on to tell me that Sherlock had had an aneurysm, which sent him into a brief coma, and as he was coming out, he kept calling my name.

"He's calling for you so much," Naomi said. "The doctor thinks it would be a good idea if you came here to the hospital."

I could tell that Naomi hated having to ask me that, but I was as upset as she was. All of a sudden, I started thinking about Sherlock when he'd gone to Mexico. And the night that he'd returned and how I'd wanted to hurt him then. I was having flashbacks to how hurt I'd been and I hung up and told Naomi that I would get back to her.

When I first hung up the phone, I didn't want to go. Sherlock had hurt me so much and I didn't know why I had to help him now. But as I prayed, I asked God to give me the courage to do the right thing. I knew that I was supposed to forgive Sherlock and this was a test of my faith. God moved me and my heart and I went to be by Sherlock's side.

He recovered, of course, and we went on living our lives separately, though Sherlock was never too far away from me.

I enjoyed living in that townhouse. It was probably one of the most stable times of my life as far as where I was living, but my employment situation was a different story. I had several jobs during those years. I worked for the Community Relations Department and then, Occupational Training Center, and after that, several other places. I was going from job to job, not because I wanted to, but so many of my positions were federally funded programs and once the money ran out, my job would be gone.

But it wasn't just that some programs expired. I left a few jobs because I couldn't manage my responsibilities because of my eyesight. So a couple of times, I left before I was fired. I left because of my failing eyesight.

Financially, it became a tough time for me. Trying to stay afloat, trying to maintain my home, trying to make all ends meet when I wasn't working regularly. Plus, there was the ever-present challenge of not being able to drive. My eyesight was getting much worse, and more rapidly during this time than ever before.

My eyesight wasn't my only health challenge. I discovered that I had to have a major operation -- a hysterectomy. I'd developed fibroid tumors that were affecting my body so much, my doctor recommended the surgery.

So, I had the operation but not long after I went back to work I lost my job with the Occupational Training Center, which was another federally funded program. Of course, I applied for another job, but there just didn't seem to be any options out there for me.

After a while, I even stopped applying for jobs. I was feeling so sorry for myself. I didn't have any money, and I was really going blind now. I was to the point where I could hardly see.

There were little jobs that I would do to just keep myself afloat. Things that other people might see as degrading, but I was doing whatever I had to do to take care of myself. I would stuff envelopes at home, or I'd assemble pins to convention badges and then box them up and ship them back to the company.

Thankfully, I didn't have to always do these jobs alone. My sister, Rosie, would come over to support me and we would do that all day. Between those little jobs and Social Security disability, I made enough money to manage. I didn't live well, but I got by.

# Chapter 20

After all that I'd been through, I felt like I was at my wit's end. I was feeling sorry for myself and my life felt like just pressure. . . pressure. . . pressure. I knew that if I didn't get away I was going to lose it.

I saw an ad on television about a quick getaway to Montego Bay, Jamaica. Right away, I made the decision to go. It was a spontaneous decision, but I needed to do this. My money was still really tight, but I'd just gotten a check in for a job I'd done and I decided to treat myself.

The next thing was, who was I going to get to go with me? I went through my list of friends and came up with my friend, Renee. I figured this would be good for her, since she was always having to cope with the challenges of raising four sons.

When I called her up, I went right into my spiel. "Renee, I saw this ad, and wouldn't a trip to Jamaica be great? There's this four-day trip to Jamaica. Let's get away!"

I wasn't sure how much talking I was going to have to do, but believe it or not, she was amenable right away. "Okay," she said.

And then a couple of weeks later, we were on our way.

I was so excited; I'd never been to Jamaica before and we flew down on Air Jamaica. When we landed, we were greeted by the tour guide staff who took us on one of those little buses from the airport to the hotel.

The hotel was located in Montego and the beach was just a block away. There were lots of activities in and around the hotel.

We settled into our room, but we didn't want to stay there long. We just went to freshen up before we went to dinner. Most of the restaurants were on the second floor of the hotel, and we stopped at one to check out the menus.

"Oh, this looks good," Renee said, as she looked at the menu that was placed outside. It was dim in the restaurant so of course, I couldn't see well. "Let me tell you what they have."

Just as she started to read the selections, this guy walked up to us.

"Well, good evening, ladies."

"Hello," Renee and I said at the same time.

I could tell from the direction of his voice that he was kind of short.

He kept on, "Let me tell you where you must dine." He gave us the name of the restaurant and then said, "Because they have the best red snapper."

I was thinking that sounded good. "Thank you," I said. "We'll check that out."

"Do that."

His tone let me know that he was smiling and then, Renee and I just walked away. We wanted to explore what was in the other restaurants, but we did end up going to the one that had been recommended to us.

And like the man had told us, the red snapper was so good. This was a fabulous way for us to spend our first night in Jamaica -- a relaxing time with great food. But as we were leaving, we ran into that gentleman again.

"Well, ladies, we meet again."

"Yes," Renee and I said together. And I wondered, what was this guy doing? Stalking us?

He said, "I know you enjoyed your dinner and I have another recommendation for you.

There's a fabulous show upstairs on the top floor. There's a Jamaican singer and she's awesome. You will enjoy the show."

I thanked him and told him that we were going to walk around for a little while. "But perhaps we'll come later," I said.

Renee and I went into the bathroom to freshen up a little, and once we were alone, I said to her, "What's up with that little Jewish guy and what does he want to do with us?"

Renee laughed. "Evie, he's not Jewish. At least, I don't think he is because he's black."

"Really?" I was shocked by that. His tone, the way he spoke, that's what I thought.

We laughed about that and then decided that we would check out the show that he told us about. So, we went to the top floor and when we stepped up to the maitre'd, he said, "Good evening, ladies. I already have a seat for you," as if he knew who we were.

"Huh?" I said under my breath.

But Renee and I followed him and as he escorted us, Renee started whispering, "Oh, it's with them. The guy from the restaurant."

"What?"

By this time, we were at the table and Renee and I just sat down. The man who had come up to us at the restaurant, introduced himself as Paul, and then he introduced Renee and I to his friend, one of his law partners in the firm they worked at together in Chicago.

As he finished the introductions, the waiter came by and Paul ordered Renee and I one of those island drinks.

Now, I don't drink a lot, but I knew I could handle one of those.

So, we sat there and talked and the music was getting so good. And I was feeling great because in that moment, I knew that I'd done the right thing. This was just the trip that I needed. For the first time in a long time, I was stress-free.

Even though we were sitting down, I moved with the music. I mean, it was so good, it felt like it was penetrating my soul.

And then, Paul's law partner said, "Evie, would you like to dance?"

That was such a simple question that almost made me burst into tears. I really wanted to dance, but I didn't know how to tell him that I couldn't see and that I was afraid to get out there.

So, I just told him, "No, thanks."

Thank God, he wasn't offended and we just sat there and talked as we waited for the show to begin.

And then, Paul ordered another round of drinks.

Inside, I moaned. I was having a great time, but another drink?

Renee whispered to me, "Are you okay?"

"Yeah," I whispered back. "This time, I'm gonna sip slowly." We both chuckled when I said that. But, I meant it. This second drink had to be it for me.

A few minutes after that, the show began and just like Paul had promised, it was just perfect. I enjoyed the singing, the drinks, the atmosphere. It was a wonderful night.

The singer was on the stage for about an hour and then, the club played more music after that. During the show, Paul's other three law partners came down and sat at the table next to ours. Now, we were all talking and as we did, I was still moving to the music. Getting my dance on in my seat.

One of Paul's partners said to me, "Hey, I see

you moving and enjoying the music. Why don't you dance? Come on and dance with me."

I said, "I would love to, but I'm blind."

"You been smoking gonge?" he replied.

The hairs rose on the back of my neck. I was so insulted. "I beg your pardon," I said.

"I was just asking."

"No. I cannot see," I said, my voice firm. "I'm blind."

And he didn't hesitate for a moment before he said, "Come on, I got you. You can dance. Come on. I have you."

I don't know what made me do it, but even though I felt like he'd just insulted me, I got up.

Before I moved away from the table, Renee tapped me and said, "I'm watching you. You'll be okay."

As I followed him to the dance floor, he told me his name was Leon and then, the two of us just danced. And danced and danced. I was having such a good time and so was Leon, it seemed.

He leaned over and said, "You're a great dancer."

"Thank you."

Then, Leon asked me, "What's wrong with your eyes?"

"I have an eye disease, Retinitis Pigmentosa."

"Oh," was all he said. And we just kept dancing.

I felt so safe being out there with him. It was okay because he was so caring, so compassionate. The second song came on, and the third, and then when a slow song came on, we stayed on the dance floor.

As he held me, he asked, "What is your wildest fantasy?"

What! I screamed inside my head. I had all kinds of questions about why was he asking me that? But all I said to him was, "Excuse me?"

"Well," he began as if he'd just asked an ordinary question, "you're blind, you say. So, what would you like to do?"

"I don't know how to answer that. I'd really have to think about it."

When the song was over, he escorted me back to my table and instead of going back to the table next to ours, he pulled up a chair and sat with us. We had a chance to all talk for a little while longer, but then, not long after that, the club was closing.

Leo said, "Let's go over to the pub. We can sit and talk there for a while."

I could tell that Renee just wasn't sure, so, we excused ourselves and went to the restroom to freshen up...and to talk.

Inside the restroom, I told Renee, "I think we can do it. I think these guys are safe. They're all attorneys and they're not going to risk their reputations over some ladies all the way down here in Jamaica." I kept encouraging her. "We'll be right here in the hotel, in public. We'll be okay."

Renee agreed and we went back to the club. When they asked if we were ready to go, I said, "Yes!"

Leon walked up to me, put his elbow out and said, "Grab a wing."

His actions, those words were so profound. And, I just comfortably took his elbow and we walked together. It felt so natural holding onto him. When we came to a step, he would stop and we would step down together. It was perfect.

In the pub, we continued to talk and laugh and it was the perfect end to an already great evening. When we all decided to leave, Leon walked Renee and I to our room, we said goodnight and that was it.

That was our first day, and our first night. And to me, the trip had already been worth it.

# Chapter 21

The next morning, I got a call -- at six am.

When I answered, Leon greeted me with enthusiasm. "Ever, I had a great time last night. Would you like to come over, have breakfast and go for a swim with us?"

When I hesitated, he added, "It's not just the men here. We have lots of staff here, too. You know what? Let me let you speak to one of them."

Before I could say anything, he put a woman on the phone. "Hi, Ever. My name is Janella," she said in her wonderful island accent. "And I just want you to know that it's safe here."

"Okay," I said, and she put Leon back on the phone. Then, I asked him, "What time is the swim?"

"I can come and get you now, or I can wait around."

"Well, I'm just waking up. So what about seven to seven-thirty."

"You gotta do it before the sun comes up, Evie!"

"Okay." So, I got up, but right away Renee told me that she wasn't going. I understood that -- she was married and I wasn't. But then, I began to wonder...did I really want to do this by myself?

After thinking about it, though, I told Renee, "I'm going to go. I feel like it's safe."

"Well then, go and have a good time," she told me.

Like he promised, Leon came to the room, picked me up, and we went over to his villa and went for a swim. But it wasn't easy as I thought it would be. When I got there, I was a bit nervous. I'd learned how to swim, but I didn't know this pool.

Still, I got in. And wouldn't you know it, a couple of minutes later, I swam to the deep end and panicked. At first, Leon thought I was playing, but then, he grabbed me and helped me out of the pool. As I sat at the side, Janella rushed over to make sure I was okay. She brought me towels, and got me covered up. They were all so concerned that I was all right.

So then, we had breakfast there at the pool

and that's when Leon told me that this was going to be their last full day in Jamaica. "So, I want to take you guys around the island and show you a few things."

"Let me call Renee and tell her so she'll be ready."

After I showered and changed into the clothes that I'd brought with me, Leon and I picked up Renee and then he took us on a tour of Jamaica as he knew it. Even though my sight was hampered, I could feel the beauty. One of the most enjoyable places was Negril. There he introduced us to several people on that island and we had a late lunch at a place called The Bus, which was a bus now turned into a spot where delicious Jerk Chicken was sold. The Bus had become really famous with tourists. He also took us to a small shack and purchased a wood carved elephant for me (The beginning of my elephant collection). He introduced me to one particular man who he said he'd known for the years he'd been traveling to Jamaica.

"This is a special friend of mine," Leon told the man. "And she's going blind."

"I have something for you," the man said. He

went to the back of his shack and returned with something. "Feel this," he said, putting some kind of figure into my hands. "Tell me what it is."

So, I let my hands travel over the carvings and finally I said, "Is this an elephant?"

"Yes. And it's yours. You'll have good luck for the rest of your life."

That was so special to me.

"Wait a minute," he said. "I have something else."

Leon described to me that the man took off his shirt and dived right into the ocean. A few minutes later, he returned with a beautiful shell. "I want you to have this."

"Thank you," I said, hugging this man who had given me two wonderful gifts. I couldn't believe he'd been so kind.

Leon continued taking us around the island, pointing out the shops that we should go to. I did a bit of shopping that day; I ended up buying another elephant, a very nice carving. It was a full day of touring the island, and again, it was wonderful.

The next morning, Leon called me early again, and said, "I want to take you and Rene to another place in Negril before I head out. All of us are going."

Renee and I agreed to go with them. There was a reason why Leon wanted me to take that ride with him was because he wanted us to see where he was planning to build a hotel...the Ebony Inn. It was going to be a small hotel, with only about eighteen rooms.

"This has always been a dream of mine," he said when we got to the land where he was going to develop his hotel. "I've always wanted a place like this in Jamaica."

I was so happy for Leon. This was going to be an incredible project for him. He was developing his dream.

I returned home ready to face new challenges; after an exciting and rewarding weekend.

I had been able to clear my head while on that trip and was therefore able to make a monumental decision. I decided to let Victor live with Sherlock full-time. There was always so much back and forth drama between Sherlock and I and I knew that it was only so that my-ex could stay in my life. I couldn't take it anymore; it was driving me crazy. So, I finally let go and told Sherlock, "You keep him. You take care of Victor."

It was hard for me to do that, but I really thought it was best. Not just for me, but for Victor, too. The school he would be going to if he lived with his father was better. Victor was young and didn't need to spend his time taking care of me and my failing eyesight. And of course, Sherlock would be gone out of my life. All of the drama would stop.

But I was so wrong. Because any time Sherlock Houston was around, there was always more drama to come.

# Chapter 22

I honestly thought that I was doing what was best for my son. I was not in a good place financially, especially since Sherlock wasn't giving me child support. Of course, I could've taken Sherlock to court and forced him, but I didn't want to do that. It wasn't my style.

So the best thing for Victor was to be with Sherlock. His father could provide a better lifestyle for him. That's what I truly believed.

And Victor would have plenty of company over at his father's house. Besides Sherlock and Naomi, Sherlock's oldest son (from a relationship prior to our marriage) and his two children were there. His son's wife had passed away from asthma, and so Sherlock had a house full of folks, which I thought could be good for Victor.

But just because my son and I weren't in the same household, didn't mean that our connection was broken. Every morning before Victor left for school, I would call him. That in itself was an ordeal.

I had to call Sherlock's house and Naomi would always answer.

"Hello."

"Hi, may I talk to Victor, please."

That always made me cringe, but never stopped me from making the call. And then, when he got home from school, just about every day, Victor would ride his bicycle down to my townhouse.

But if I thought Victor living with Sherlock would stop my ex-husband from being in my life, I was wrong. Whenever Sherlock knew that Victor was with me, he'd stop by and drop off his two grandchildren with me, too. So now, instead of just feeding Victor, I was feeding Sherlock's seven and nine-year-old grandchildren as well.

Besides those three, there were times when I had another little girl from the neighborhood. I'd met a woman who lived in the complex, not too far from me. She and her husband worked full time, so I would keep their daughter, Caitlan, after school to earn a little extra money.

So, I had a full house, but I was smart about making inexpensive meals. I'd make dinners that were always inexpensive and easy to prepare: spaghetti, macaroni casserole. Meals that fill them up and go far, too.

I'd only have the children for an hour or two, and honestly, I loved having them all there. I would load them up with food and as much love as I could give them until Sherlock and Naomi would come and pick them up.

That time was so ironic to me. With Victor living with his father, Sherlock was supposed to be out of my life. But there just didn't seem to be any way that I could get rid of him. My girlfriends and I would talk about that all the time. No matter what I'd do, I couldn't get Sherlock out of my life. That just seemed to be a fact that I had to live with.

Another fact that I had to live with was my eyesight. I'd contacted the New Jersey State Commission for the Blind because my sight had deteriorated so much. I was now using a cane and the commission gave me mobility lessons. Even with that, I wasn't feeling totally secure with the cane, though I would walk around my apartment building trying to get used to the cane. It was hard because I felt such shame carrying it. But there was nothing I could do. I knew that I had to just accept this.

And then, I was called in for a job interview. Finally! After being out of work for two years, I got an interview with the Department of Health and Human Services.

I was excited to finally have a prospective job and I was determined to have a good interview. I was determined to put my best foot forward. But I had one dilemma: should I take my cane or not take my cane? I didn't think long about it -- I decided it would be best for me to have the cane.

My interview was held at an agency called, StepUp, which was in Camden, New Jersey.

I walked into the receptionist area and spoke to the young woman there. "My name is Ever Lee Hairston and I'm here to apply for the position as a counselor. My interview is with Dr. Phillips."

She directed me to his office. "Go up the steps and when you get to the top of the steps, make a right and he's straight across in that office." She paused. "I'll call up and let him know that you're on your way."

I did exactly what she said; and having the

cane with me helped. I found the office and in just a few minutes, I was sitting in front of Dr. Phillips.

He told me a little about the position and then, he asked me to tell him a little about myself.

"Well, I taught school when I first graduated from college and I left that position. I could no longer teach because of my eyesight."

"Well, with your eyesight, how are you going to do this job?"

"I don't know yet," I said, right away. "But, I'm gonna figure it out. Because I'm never giving up another job again because of my eyesight. I have four other senses that I can use."

Dr. Phillips was quiet for a moment, and so was I. I had spoken those words, but I was just as surprised by what I'd said as the doctor was. I hadn't planned to say that; that's just what came out and I thought that statement was so profound.

Then, Dr. Phillips said, "You just seem so much more qualified than this position."

"But I need to start somewhere," I told him. "I have to and I know that I can do this."

I could tell that he was really considering

everything that I was saying. But, he still had his doubts. "You know, in this position, seeing a person's body language is really important."

"Yes, I do believe that. But like I said, I have learned to use my others senses to compensate for my loss of eyesight. I use my other senses better than my eyes." I paused. "For example, you just crossed your legs."

I could sense the doctor was smiling.

I said, "I could tell because my hearing is more sensitive. Auditory clues are just as effective."

"Ever Lee Hairston, you got the job."

"Thank you!"

"Now, you'll have to find a way to take notes."

"That won't be a problem. I can print really well and I'll be able to do it."

"Okay. You can start on Monday."

I walked out of there, with my cane, feeling so good about what I'd just demonstrated to the doctor and to myself.

And on that following Monday, I was back there to begin my first day as a counselor-trainee. It was clear that the department had never had a blind employee before. I couldn't see well enough to say that everyone was staring at me, but I could feel it.

But I handled that job, and I handled it well. I got to the point where I would sit with the client, interview them, write the notes, and then the secretary would type the notes out for me.

It was a good time in my life because I didn't even have to deal with Sherlock too much. Judy decided that I didn't need to depend on Sherlock to drive me to and from work. So, she drove me to work in the mornings and then, we found a driver who took me home at night. We found a way to work it all out.

From the moment I told Dr. Phillips that I was never going to give up another job because of my eyesight, I was determined to make that the truth. I was determined to live a full life and learn how to live well.

I was surrendering...surrendering to the inevitable. It was going to happen, I was going to be blind.

For the first time, I truly understood what Dr. King meant when he said, "Free at last," because by surrendering, that was finally me.

# Chapter 23

I was really excited about my new job at the Department of Health and Human Services.

Every morning Dr. Phillips had a staff session where we'd review the clients that we had in our division, which was for alcohol and substance abuse. It only took me a few weeks to be able to sit in that meeting and give Dr. Phillips the feedback that he was looking for. I was insightful, on top of my clients, and was able to stay on target.

As I sat in those meetings, I thought about how I'd gotten here and all that I'd been through, from giving up my career as a teacher in 1968 because of my eyesight, to trying to find another job, and then running as soon as the people at the new job found out I was blind, to then going through the whole process again. All of these years had been such as struggle for me.

But here I was in this job that just seemed to be such a great fit. I loved working with the clients, teaching alcohol and drug education classes, and then meeting with and counseling the clients afterward. It felt like I had a gift to do this and it didn't take me long to feel like this was the place where I needed to be.

Sometimes while I sat in those meetings, feeling for the first time in a long time like I really belonged, I'd just start praying inside, thanking God for placing me in a career where I was useful, where I was needed. I thanked Him for giving me the skills where I would be able to make a positive difference in someone else's life.

I knew that I was progressing well, but I was still surprised when a few months after I started, Dr. Phillips called me into his office. "Ever Lee," he began, "you're doing a great job."

"Thank you."

"I'd like to see you go further. Now, because of the situation, we had to start you at the very bottom, but what I'd like now is for you to start taking classes so that you can continue to be promoted with the County. They're being held all around Trenton and New Brunswick and most of these classes the County will pay for."

"Okay, great," I agreed.

I was really excited about advancing, but when I walked out of Dr. Phillips' office I did have a question: How would I do this? My blindness had progressed to the point where I knew that if a professor was giving a lecture and would write on the board, I wouldn't be able to see it at all.

But just like with everything else in my life, I came up with a solution -- I decided that I would record the classes. My friends thought that was a great idea and Tina, really had a great idea.

"Ever Lee, I'm going to donate something to you."

And a few weeks later, she gave me a cassette recorder.

Even Sherlock helped out. He would buy me cases of Memorex tapes from one of those supermarket warehouses, so I never had to be concerned about that.

The classes were usually held two days out of the month, and there were three of us from the job taking the classes, so I always had a ride. For the first time in my career, I didn't feel any pressure. I was hired as a blind person, everyone knew I was blind, so I didn't have to do anything to try to hide it. That really took a lot of stress off of me and allowed me to perform to the best of my ability.

And I did! I'd only been with the Country for about a year, when I took the Civil Service Exam. Not only did I pass the test, but I was number one. The County worked it out for me because obviously, I couldn't read the test and I didn't know Braille. So, someone read the test to me and I aced it.

Working it out this way, with recording my classes, having someone read the tests to me, gave me a lot of confidence. And since Victor was still living with Sherlock, I decided to use this time to take even more classes. This time I attended Rutger's University. I really wanted to get my Master's in Social Work so I registered for the classes, and then my cousin's husband, Dr. Brown, drove me to the university.

Just like with the other classes, I used those cassettes to keep up. And, I was able to do it.

One of the first classes that I had to take for my graduate degree was one of the most interesting and most memorable classes I'd ever taken. It was 'Death and Dying.' The focus of the class was about the difference of emotions one may experience in a sudden death versus a prolonged, terminal illness that leads to death.

It may have seemed like a strange class, but it had a profound effect on me. I could relate to the lectures because of my sister, Rebecca. And as I sat in there, listening to the lectures week after week, something began to happen to me -- I began to really heal.

It had been twenty years since Rebecca had died, and I didn't realize until then that I'd never gotten over her death. Her passing had been so hard on me, since she was the sibling I was closest to growing up. It wasn't until I sat in that class that I realized I was still filled with grief.

But in that classroom, I healed. I learned to deal with the feelings of guilt that I still had, wondering if I could've done more to help her, and even wondering if I'd done anything to hurt her.

I know it made no sense that I'd been feeling that way, but grief rarely makes sense. I'd always wondered if I'd made my sister's illness any worse by keeping our bedroom window open.

Let me explain -- Rebecca and I slept in the

same bed, and I always wanted to have the window open -- even just a little. I had to, because I could hardly breathe. It was because of my allergies; and between the oil burner that was in our bedroom and my father smoking, it was hard for me. So, I would want the window opened just a little bit.

But Rebecca who was always sick would tell me, "Ever Lee, close that window."

"But Becky, I can't breathe," is what I would tell her.

Then, she would call out to our father, "Dad, Ever Lee has the window open!"

And my father would say, "Close that window!"

Of course, I would close it, but later, when I was sleeping, I'd almost always wake up, not able to breathe. So, I'd do it again; I'd open the window.

And Becky would wake up. Then, she called out, "Dad!"

And it would start all over again.

That was the only time in my life that I got spanked by my dad. One night, my father came into the room and spanked me because not only had I disobeyed him, but because my parents and grandparents were so concerned about keeping the heat in, especially since oil was so expensive.

As I sat in that class, that incident played over and over in my mind and I didn't even realize that inside I'd been asking myself that question for years. But hearing the lectures allowed me to make peace and let it go. The truth was Rebecca was ill and her death was just something that happened. There was nothing that I'd done to cause it, nor could I have prevented it.

I took other classes at Rutgers, too. When I'd passed the Civil Service Exam, that was so that I could stay employed with the County. But, I had to be certified, too. Certification helped us to maintain our positions. So, I took summer classes at Rutgers for that.

While I was moving up in my career, my eyesight was getting worse. Of course, I was using the cane to get around. I still had some light perception, and I could see my writing if I used a large marker. I could see to write, but to refocus so that I could read was very difficult.

Getting dressed in the morning, I used skills

that I'd taught myself. I'd hold my garments under the light and I could make out light colors versus dark colors. I even did it with hosiery. I would only buy black or nude stockings. It was easier to identify the colors that way. That was the way I'd managed to dress myself appropriately.

Then in 1987, my life really had a major change.

I received a call from someone from the National Center for the Blind in Baltimore. After she told me that her name was Jackie, she said, "Ever Lee, I work as a membership developer and I got your name from the New Jersey Commission for the Blind. I wanted to invite you to come to our convention, which is going to be in Phoenix, Arizona this year. What do you think?"

I was surprised by the call, but it wasn't just my surprise that made me hesitant. I loved my job. And, I didn't think I would be able to just take off from work and go to this convention that was clear across the country. "I'm not sure," I told Jackie. "I'm not sure about getting time off from my job."

"Well, see if you can. I think you'll really enjoy it and the information you'll receive is so valuable."

I told her I would think about it, but I was really apprehensive about asking for permission to have time off for this. But after a couple of days, I decided to do it. Something just kept driving me to ask for the time off. And, they gave it to me.

So, I was off to Phoenix. Interestingly enough, I had no concerns about traveling by myself even though my sight was failing. I'd been to New York as a young girl by myself, so I guess I figured that I could do anything after that.

The flight from Philadelphia to Phoenix was uneventful, and catching a cab to the hotel was easy enough.

But then, I walked into that hotel and everything changed. There was a mob of people, all blind, of course. It was loud and all around me, I could hear the canes tapping. As I eased my way through the crowd to get to the front desk, I was accidentally poked by canes, my legs were licked by dogs and I wondered what had I gotten myself into?

It took me a moment, but I finally got to the front desk and checked-in. That was when I found out that I was sharing a room with Jackie, the woman who'd invited me and another lady.

When I walked into the room, they sure made me feel welcomed. Jackie said, "I'm so glad that you decided to come, Ever Lee, you're going to have a good time." Then right as I put my bags down, Jackie said, "We were just waiting for you, but there's a buffet downstairs and it's a good deal. They reduced the rate for our group, so you wanna go?"

"Okay." That was fine with me after the long, long plane ride. I was starving.

But it wasn't until I actually got in the buffet line that I asked myself, 'What in the world?' I mean, how are these people doing it? How were they choosing their food and putting it on their plates? Whatever they were doing, they did it better than me because my first time through that buffet line was not a good experience. I stuck my fingers in the mashed potatoes, and then a second later, I was using the gravy as a finger bowl. I just didn't know how these people did this.

I finally made it through that line and sat down with Jackie and my other roommate. But we could hardly chat. The two of them knew so many people and they introduced me to everyone. I had never met so many people at one time before.

That networking continued throughout the weekend. Jackie introduced me to the new president of the Federation, all of the board members, and the directors of the schools that were under the direction of the National Federation of the Blind.

And not only did I meet so many people, but I learned the Federation's philosophy that it's respectable to be blind and how the Federation wanted to change what it meant to be blind. I listened as everyone talked about how the Federation acted as a vehicle for collective self-expression for the blind. And the Federation had been around for such a long time; since 1940, it had been working toward the goal of helping blind persons achieve self-confidence and self-respect. They believed in the complete integration of the blind into society on the basis of equality.

I went to bed excited. I'd never been around so many positive and professional blind people before. It was the best medicine for me, and it felt like I was on the verge of a whole different life.

The next morning, when I went down to the registration table, I had to wait in one of the long, long lines. But, I didn't mind. Standing there, I met new people, chatted and learned about their lives, heard about their experiences, and learned what being blind meant to them.

When I finally made my way to the table, the lady asked, "What's your name?"

I told her, and it was a simple process because Jackie had already registered me.

Then, the lady asked, "Would you like a Braille or a print agenda?"

Her question stopped me in my tracks and took my breath away. Braille or print?

I guessed that was a good question because I could no longer read print, but I hadn't been taught Braille.

A light bulb went off for me. My eyes filled with tears and I don't know why after everything that I'd been through, that this was the moment when I realized this was all real. I guess it was because I was standing there and I couldn't give the lady an answer. Truly, I wouldn't be able to read either form. I was a college grad, yet I was illiterate.

But what that moment did for me, is that it made me eager to learn everything that I needed to know as a blind person. When I told Jackie this, she introduced me to Joanne Wilson, the director of the Louisiana Center for the Blind. I told her my story from childhood to where I was now. And I told her, how I felt, not being able to even read the agenda.

"Oh, honey," she said. "You just need to get some skills. You just need to come down to Louisiana, get this training and you'll be fine." Then, she told me about the Center, which had been started just two years before in 1985 and she explained the type of training they did. They taught real life skills for the blind and I knew right then that I had to get down there.

The challenge was, they wanted you at the Center for at least six months, and they actually preferred nine months. How would I be able to get away from work for that long? I had no idea, but I really hoped that I'd be able to figure it out.

On my third day at the convention, I was walking from the convention hall back to the hotel and a young lady came up to me. "Hi," she said, "you look a little lost."

"Well, I'm new, this is my first time here."

"Oh, well, I can help you. My name is Christina, by the way," she said. I told her that I was Ever Lee and then she said, "I'm high partial; how much vision do you have?"

From that moment, we connected. That night, we sat and talked and the next day, I met her mom and dad and spent some time with them. But, I couldn't stay for the whole convention. I had to get back to work.

"But promise we'll stay in touch," Tina said.

I made that promise and we did stay in touch.

I returned to New Jersey, inspired and encouraged. I'd never met so many blind people before and it felt good to know that I was not alone. I was also motivated to go to that Center in Louisiana, but I couldn't see that happening. So, I just took the things I'd learned from the long weekend and settled in back at home, very, very happy that I'd made the trip.

# Chapter 24

It was 1988. I had been working for a couple of years now, and even though my eyesight was failing, I felt like I was doing better. I was in a good place in my life and decided this was the time to make a move. I bought my first home, a three-bedroom townhouse with a full basement.

Buying a home just made more sense than continuing to rent because the rent just kept going up and up. And as it turned out, my mortgage was less than the rent I was paying.

And the best part of getting that house...Victor came back to live with me.

I didn't plan it that way. Of course, when I bought the house, I made sure that there was a room for my son. And I told him, "Victor, any time you come over, this will be your room."

My son didn't hesitate when he said, "I really want to move in with you."

"You can. Of course, you can," I told him.

So Victor moved back home with me and I

was thrilled to have him back. It was such a good time because now that I had a home, family could come to visit. I had more than enough room. The first floor was complete with a large living and dining room, a full sit-in kitchen and a den. There was also a bathroom downstairs. Upstairs, there were two bedrooms, an office, and another bathroom. And then, I had the full basement. I was so happy to have that house and it was always filled with people whether they were visiting or I was just entertaining for the day.

And then, that summer, I returned for my second convention.

Just like we promised, Christina and I had kept in touch and so we had made plans to room together. Not only did I feel like we were good friends, but I learned a lot from Christina. Not skills, because she didn't have a lot of skills. But I learned valuable lessons about knowing people, and getting around, and doing things, and being free as a blind person.

Christina and I even went to a dance the first night we were there, and I got out on the floor...and danced! It was so freeing getting out and doing things that I never ever imagined that I could do as a blind person. It was enlightening, exciting, and encouraging.

This convention felt so much more social to me. Maybe it was because it was my second one or maybe it was because of Christina. But we just hung out. After the banquet, some of the people had parties in their rooms, and we went from room to room, from party to party. I felt like I was living a normal life. Living like my sighted friends lived. I was doing what they did. The only difference -- I was doing it with blind people. It was a fabulous convention.

And the good times just continued for me. I returned home and the following year, in 1989, Victor graduated from high school.

Of course, I had to share this wonderful moment for Victor with Sherlock and Naomi. But that was fine. That's just the way life was. I wasn't going to give up spending any time with my son, so that just meant that we had to do these things all together.

I wasn't able to see Victor walk across the stage, but that didn't stop me from being proud when they called his name. It was one of the proudest moments of my life. I was so happy, but at the same time, I was sad. It was bittersweet because Victor had already told me he was going to college in California. From the time he got to high school, he and his best friend, Myles had decided that California was where they wanted to be.

By the time Victor was a senior, he had it all figured out. "Mom, I've got it mapped out," he said. "Now, I know you don't have the money, but this is what we're going to do."

I sat there as my son laid out the plan.

"I'm going to Santa Barbara City College, become a resident of California, and then, I'll be able to get my education for free. All you'll have to do is provide me with room and board."

So that's what Victor and Myles did. That summer, they left for California. It was going to be such an adventure for them. And it was the beginning of a new journey for me as well.

# Chapter 25

One of my responsibilities working at the Department of Health and Human Services was going to the high schools and giving Alcohol and Drug Education seminars for the teachers at Burlington High School. The seminars focused on teaching the symptoms of abuse, so that the teachers would be aware and would be able to identify any issues among their students. It was such a natural fit for me since I'd been a teacher.

I'd been teaching at Burlington for a few months when one afternoon during the lunch break, I was standing by my desk, trying to decide what I was going to do. I hadn't really brought anything for lunch, though I always had something like a yogurt with me.

I was pondering whether or not I would just eat that when I felt someone approach me. I couldn't really see him, but I heard his footsteps coming toward me.

Then, he stopped, and said, "Wow, you are

different!"

I had no idea what he meant by that. I said, "Excuse me?"

He said, "I've stared, I've waved, I've tried everything that I can think of to get your attention and I couldn't. But now, that I have it, my name is Theodore Dow."

"Oh, well, my name is Ever. And I'm sorry. I really didn't see you; I'm blind."

"Oh!" I could tell that my words had surprised him. "Well, how much do you see?"

"I have some light perception, not much, though. I really couldn't see you."

"That's interesting," he said. "Let me give you my card because I teach computer workshops here and I'm interested in doing something with the blind."

"That would be great," I said.

"I hope you'll give me a call because I really want to do this."

"Okay," I said casually, not making any kind of commitment at all.

He walked away without me giving him my number, and I never did call him back, nor did I see him at Burlington High again.

A few months later, a new computer school moved into the high rise building where I worked and as I was walking down the hall one day, I heard Theodore's voice.

He stopped me and said, "Hi, remember me?" Then after a short pause, he added, "Wait, that's right, you can't see me. I'm the gentleman that you talked to over at Camden High School."

"Oh, how're you doing?"

"I'm good. I was listening to your lecture in the classroom because you're right across the hall from me. I work for that new computer school that just moved in."

"Wow, that's interesting."

"I love what I do, but I really enjoyed listening to you speak. I hope that since we're in the same building, we'll be able to have lunch one day."

"Maybe we can. But right now, I'm in a hurry. I have to get upstairs to my director's office," I told him.

"Then, I'll see you around."

Another week or two passed and I ran into Theodore once again. And just like the last time, he asked me to lunch. But this time, I said yes.

"What about one o'clock?" I asked him. "I'll be free then, will that work for you?"

"Yes, definitely. Great!"

So, we went to the restaurant that was on the first floor of the building. I just had a soup and sandwich and really had a pleasant time. I found out that Theodore was a retired school teacher, a principal, actually. And now, he taught these computer classes.

After lunch, I checked up on him a little bit, asking people that I knew who might also know Theodore. I ran into one of my church members, an acquaintance who worked in Theodore's office. I told her how I'd met him and I asked, "What do you think of him?"

"He's a really nice guy, Evie. Really, really nice. I think you should give him a chance. You need to go out anyway. Get out and do something."

I appreciated her enthusiasm, but I wasn't so interested in going out. I was still more focused on getting some training and building up my skills.

But I did give him a chance and we went out on a couple of dates. I found out that he was quite a bit older than me -- twelve years to be exact, and he'd been married before and had adult children. He'd retired from the armed services before he began teaching. I met his family -- his children, and brothers and sisters, and we just hung out whenever we had the chance.

One thing that we talked a lot about were my plans to go to the Louisiana Center so that I could learn alternative life skills to become more independent as a blind person.

He was really supportive and took an interest in my doing that.

"Whatever I can do to help you to make that happen, Evie, just let me know."

I was already determined to go to Louisiana, but with Theodore encouraging me, too, I started to push to make that happen. It wasn't going to be easy to get that much leave from my job. The County had never granted anyone a leave to go to school. Not that the County wasn't supportive of education -- they were. It was just that employees used nights and weekends to do that. To have someone completely away from their job -- that part had never been done before.

But with the few political ties I had, I was finally able to make that happen and I was granted a three-month leave to go to Louisiana. I was told that three months was all that they were able to give me...and I took it, even though I knew that the Center wanted me to be there for a minimum of six months. But, I took the three months and figured that I would just work the rest of it out later.

When I was finally able to square things away at my job, I think Theodore was as excited as I was.

"What can I do to help you, Evie? I really want to help you with whatever you need."

I was pretty sure that I was going to figure out a way to stay at the Center the entire time and I didn't want my house to be sitting all that time. So I knew I needed to figure out something with my place.

Theodore had a couple of houses in Philadelphia that he owned, and as I got to know him, I really felt like I could trust him. Plus, he'd come highly recommended by my friend, so I decided to ask him if he would watch my house while I was away.

He agreed that he would go over there at least once a week, to check out the house, water my plants, and do anything else that was needed.

But the biggest thing that Theodore did for me, was when I told him that I was going to Louisiana, he told me that he was going to drive me there.

"We'll drive you," he said. "Me and my brother."

"That's a long ride. Are you sure?"

"Of course, no problem. I'll be glad to do that. I told you, whatever I can do to help you make this happen, I will."

I was so grateful for that because I hadn't really thought about how I was going to get to Louisiana. And, I certainly didn't want to ask Sherlock. I didn't want Sherlock involved in any way.

So Theodore, his brother and I got into their car in October of 1990 and headed toward Louisiana. We didn't make the whole trip at once -- we made one stop in North Carolina, at my Mom and Dad's house and we spent the night there.

I prepared my parents for our arrival, just

telling them that Theodore was a man I'd met, who was being kind to me, and he was an overall good guy. So that my parents wouldn't be concerned, I told them that I'd met Theodore's family and he was just a very nice man.

And so, he met my parents and the next day, we arrived in Louisiana.

"I'm rooting for you, Evie," he told me. "I'll take care of everything back home, don't you worry. You just do what you have to do down here. And I'll be there when you get back."

# Chapter 26

It was in 1987 at my first convention when Joanne Wilson first told me about the Louisiana Center, and now, three years later, I was finally able to make this happen. Victor was away in college, so this was really the perfect time. I'd been motivated by the conventions and all the blind professional people I was meeting and I really wanted to learn the alternative life skills that I knew would add even more quality to my life. I wanted to receive all the proper training to be able to compete with my sighted colleagues.

This was the first time that I would be living with people who were blind. Of course, I grew up with my sister, but like I've said before, there was very little communication about our eyesight.

From the moment Theodore and his brother dropped me off at the Center in Ruston, Louisiana, I loved it. It was like a small campus with an Administrative Building, which was the hub of the campus. The classes were held in that building along with the kitchen where we had our cooking classes. There was also a library, which was an all-purpose room. We used that room for graduations and the graduation meals. And of course, there was a computer room.

Then, there were the dormitories where we lived, two-bedroom apartments where we each had roommates. But the roommates were not at the same levels. It was designed so that if you were new, you were assigned a roommate who was a little ahead of you. Someone who could pass on what they'd learned. Someone who could mentor you.

My roommate was Loretta, a young woman from McAuthor, Louisiana, who was the mother of two. She was the perfect roommate for me, so caring, compassionate, and encouraging to me. Knowing how far Loretta had come, gave me hope that I could do the same thing.

We were on a schedule that began early in the morning when we had to get up and walk to the Administration Building. We met in the reception area every morning for a staff meeting and then twice a week, we attended seminars where we discussed blindness, blindness issues, and how we would solve challenges.

It was like being in school again. I was learning something new every day, learning things that sighted people took for granted, but were challenging for us. Like learning how to go to the grocery store by myself, learning how to set up my kitchen, and how to label my seasonings so that I didn't always have to smell them, learning how to travel on a bus.

We had a class called Mobility and Orientation where we learned how to find an address. And after we were taught this, we would go on what the teachers called, Drop-Offs where they would take us in the van somewhere, drop us off and tell us to find the mall. Of course we had Braille classes and basic living trips like going to a restaurant.

I loved it all. I was trying to just take it all in and soak it all up because I didn't know how long I was going to be there. I hadn't worked out my three-month stay; I hadn't figured out if I was going to be able to stay longer. So, I just worked hard and studied every night. My confidence was building. I was learning that it was okay to be blind, there was no shame in that.

The three months went by much too fast and I knew there was so much I had to learn and wanted to learn. So when it was time for me to return to work, I called my job and told them I was sick. And, I got to stay another three months. But I knew that I wouldn't get any more time than this. I was going to have to do in six months what most did in nine months, and some students even took twelve months.

So, it was all about school for me and I made it work.

The Orientation and Mobility Training were the most interesting exercises to me. They would take us out, group us into threes with one instructor, and then give us addresses that we had to find.

So, they took us out during Mardi Gras and had us walking on Bourbon Street, stepping over homeless people, passing by all kinds of folks who wanted to pray for us, do a reading for us, everything.

It was quite an adventure because so much was going on around me, I had to really stay focused. But my focus was almost broken when I heard a man singing, "Three blind mice...three blind mice...."

That was tough to hear. But surprisingly, it wasn't the lessons from the Louisiana Center that got me through that moment. It was lessons that I'd learned long ago...lessons from Dr. King.

As I walked down Bourbon Street, hearing that man singing, hearing other people shouting at us, I did what Dr. King had taught me -- I focused on the task and not the people. I was on a mission to get through this school, and there was no way that I was going to let people who I didn't know and who didn't know me, deter me in any way. It wasn't going to happen.

That Mardi Gras experience lasted for two days, and then, we were taken back to Ruston. It was a memorable time, but a time of great accomplishment for me.

Everything was passing quickly, and I was close to my time being up. But I felt like I was ready. I'd learned the lessons, I'd done the tasks, and I was ready for graduation.

But there was one major "exam" that I had to take before I could graduate, I had to take a 'graduation route' where I would be dropped off by myself and would have to make my way back to the mall.

I was assigned to Monroe, Louisiana where I would be dropped off. "You'll have to find the Transportation Center, Ever Lee," the instructor told me. "And then from there, you'll have to get to the Monroe Mall."

I was fine with that, I'd been through many drop-offs before, I'd made it through Bourbon Street. I knew that I'd make it through this. But then, the other students told me all about Monroe.

"Oh, they're prejudice down there."

"It's like down south."

"You may find the Klu Klux Klan there."

At first, I wasn't too worried about what they said. I was going to use my skills and stay focused on the task and not the people.

But then, the instructors dropped me off, and as I stood there in the middle of Monroe, Louisiana, I began to think about what the other students said. And I began to think that the instructors were crazy for just dropping me off here.

I was complaining inside my head, then, I

started crying, and lastly, I started praying, "God, please don't leave me out here with the Klu Klux Klan."

But then, I asked myself what was I doing? I had all of this training; I knew what to do. I could either think negatively or I could think positively.

So, I started walking, using my cane. I could feel the grass on the edge of the sidewalk, and I kept walking until the sidewalk turned to the right. I kept moving, using all of my orientation and mobility skills, and that's when I heard noise on my left, coming from a building. That was the first good sign -- we were allowed to ask for directions or ask for help.

I went inside and asked where was the Transportation Center.

"Go back outside and make a right, cross the street, then go up about two blocks, and there'll be a bus stop there. Cross right there," the person told me.

I was able to follow those directions easily enough, but once I got to the bus stop, I wasn't sure how I was going to get across the street. What about traffic? So, I stood there, and I waited, and waited and waited.

Finally, I decided to just do it. I waited until I didn't hear any traffic and then I crossed the street. But one thing the lady who gave me directions didn't tell me was that once I crossed, I'd be on an over-bridge. At least, that's what it felt like to me. I could hear traffic to the right of me, underneath me, it felt like it was all around me.

"Oh, my gosh! Where am I?"

I was so scared that I was shaking. But, I calmed myself and kept going. I had to do this if I wanted to graduate. I stayed focused on the task.

All of a sudden, I heard, "Miss, Miss." I wasn't sure if she was calling out to me until she added, "Hold up. Let me help you."

I could tell that she was probably calling from her car. I yelled back to her, "Thank you, but I'm performing a test. You can't help me; I have to do this on my own."

"Oh, okay."

"But just tell me...where is the Transportation Center?"

"You're almost there," she yelled out. "Just go up to the corner and make a right. It's on the right."

"Thank you."

I felt a bit better; I felt like I was almost to the finished line. And that's when I started singing one of my favorite songs to give me courage. "I sing because I'm happy. I sing because I'm free. His eye is on the sparrow. And, I know he watches me....."

I made it to the corner. And, I didn't cross. I just made the right like the lady told me to do.

And, I could hear the buses!

When I heard those buses, I was so relieved. But my task was not yet over. I had to stay focused. But, I asked and found the bus that was going to the Monroe Mall and when I got on and took a seat, that was when I felt victory. My palms may have been wet, but I had done it.

It only took a little while to get to the Monroe Mall and when I got inside, my instructor and several of the students were there waiting and to cheer me on.

I had made it! I was going to graduate! It had only taken me six months.

The last thing I had to do for graduation was cook a meal for forty people. But, after I had made it out of Monroe, I knew I could do anything. And cooking was no big deal for me because all my life, I'd been cooking for a big family. So I was ready for this.

My graduation meal: Hawaiian barbecue chicken, potato salad, string beans, and I had to make rolls and homemade ice cream...those last two were items we had to make.

I also wanted to make my mother's pound cake. She had given me her recipe and I'd put it on cassette. One of the instructors, Ruth, had told me to also Braille it out. And, I did, but I wasn't the best at reading Braille. I could write it fine, though.

Well, when I was ready to make my mother's cake, don't you know the recorder broke? I couldn't believe it. I was so upset; how in the world would I make the cake now?

But Ruth reminded me calmly, "Ever Lee, remember I told you that you had to write it in Braille, too? So, you do have a Braille copy."

Well, that experience is what helped me to gain more confidence in reading Braille.
I needed to make the cake and the only way to do it was to read the recipe in Braille.

And I did. I baked my cake...using Braille.

And I graduated.

I went back to New Jersey, just ready and anxious and excited about integrating all the skills that I'd learned. I was ready to integrate it all into my personal and professional life.

It was one of the best times of my life.

# Chapter 27

I returned to New Jersey in April, 1991 with a lot of confidence, much more confidence in myself, and what I'd be able to do now that I graduated from the Louisiana Center. My confidence helped me to really start moving up the ladder at work. I was able to pass additional Civil Service exams, which allowed me to have many more responsibilities at my job.

My social life picked up right where I had left it. Theodore and I had stayed in contact the whole time I was in Louisiana and we began dating once again. He was just a very kind man who took an interest in me. When I returned from Louisiana, he offered to do some work on my home.

"I had a chance to check out your house while you were away," he said. "There are couple of things you need, Evie. You could make some changes and really make this house very different."

I agreed because I knew my house could use

some work. There was a bit of wasted space, and other things that I knew would really improve it.

So Theodore went to work. That man had so many gifts and so many talents. He put up wood paneling in my basement, he added a bathroom and a bedroom to the basement, and he took some of that wasted space on the second floor and turned it into an office for me.

He made my house much nicer, with a lot more livable space. So, when my family came to visit, people could stay in the bedroom he added in the basement, or on the hideaway sofa in the Great Room.

And even with all of the work that he was doing on my home, Theodore worked with me, teaching me to be even more proficient on the computer.

We spent a lot of good times together and at the end of 1991, Theodore said to me, "Evie, I don't want to just see you, I don't want to just date you, I want to marry you."

And my first thought was, Oh, my gosh! Marriage?

There were so many thoughts in my head about all I'd been through with Sherlock. I didn't want to go through anything like that again. But, Theodore and I kept talking about it and the more we talked and the more I thought, the idea of marrying him began to appeal to me.

I had a dilemma, though. I didn't feel like I was really in love. I liked Theodore, cared for him, and appreciated him, but I couldn't call it love. I didn't feel anything toward him the way I had when I first married Sherlock.

But when I talked to a couple of my girlfriends about it, they kind of brushed away my concerns. Just about all of them said the same thing.

"Oh, Evie, what you had with Sherlock was not love. That was crazy love, infatuation, it was a whole lot of things, but it certainly wasn't love."

Well, with the way that Sherlock and I had ended, I couldn't argue with my friends. Maybe they were right. Maybe I was waiting to feel something that wasn't real. Maybe the good companionship and good times I had with Theodore were enough.

So, as Theodore and I continued to date, I began to feel more and more that I really wanted to marry him.

I started spending more time with Theodore and his family. His brothers and sisters lived in Philadelphia and I really enjoyed spending holidays with them. There was plenty of laughs and good conversation. It was fun just mingling with all of them.

Of course, I introduced him to Victor and he really liked him. When the two of them got together, Theodore and Victor had great conversations about the things that interested Victor.

That was one of the things I liked best about Theodore -- he was an all-around person, who could talk about anything and fit in with anyone. Not only that, he was so self-sufficient. He could cook, he could clean, he required very little maintenance; he could definitely take care of himself.

And then, he was always so helpful to me. Any time I wanted to visit my parents, he was willing to drive me to North Carolina. When my parents came to visit, Theodore was right there in the kitchen helping me to prepare for them and once they were there, he did everything to make sure they were comfortable and entertained.

He was just an all-around good guy who was intelligent, had great conversation, and he was very good-looking, too.

I had to ask myself, "Why would I want to pass this up? Did I really want to live by myself for the rest of my life?"

Yes, he was older, but he already made a great companion. We would be able to do things together, travel together. My thinking was that it made perfect sense for us to get married.

So, finally I agreed and in May, 1992, I married Theodore Dow. We had a private church ceremony, just his family and mine, and we had the reception in my huge backyard. We'd rented one of those very large tents that held well over one-hundred people and we decorated the entire space in purple and ivory. The tables were draped with ivory cloths, while the centerpieces were all purple. We had purple flowers everywhere throughout the backyard.

The entire day was beautiful and as I stood in that backyard celebrating the day, I was so happy that I'd decided to do it.

Marriage didn't change very much for us. Theodore was always with me anyway and we just continued living our lives. We still did everything together and I could see us growing old together. I really loved my life.

# Chapter 28

1995 was quite a turning point for me. For three years, Theodore and I were doing just fine and then one day while I was at work, I received a strange phone call from my credit union. The account I had there was one that I only used for my son. If Victor needed money quickly, I would go there, borrow the money, and I knew that by the end of the month, I would be able to pay the loan back.

But then on this day, I received a call from a woman saying that there was something unusual going on with the account and they wanted to check up with me with because they had gotten to know me. I'd established a pattern of payment with them.

"We know that when you normally borrow money, you pay it right back," she said. "Well, we sent you some coupons in the mail that were used, but they haven't been paid back. We just calling to make sure everything is okay."

"I don't know anything about that," I said.

And right away, I got a bad feeling. "I'll get back to you," I told the woman.

The moment I hung up, I called Theodore. He was the one who went through our mail because the mail was delivered while I was at work.

When he answered, I told him what the woman at the credit union had told me. At the end, I asked him, "Do you know anything about this? Did any coupons come in the mail?"

"Uh, yeah....yeah...I think they came," he stammered.

There was just something about the way Theodore answered me, something about his tone that I knew was not good. Maybe it was just that I was already suspicious about everything. After living with Sherlock, that's just the way I was.

Then after a couple of more moments of silence, he said, "Evie, we did get those coupons and I cashed them in. But, I'm going to pay it back."

"Why didn't you tell me? Why didn't you say something to me?"

Theodore didn't say anything, he didn't

answer me. I was so upset by that. I hung up and had a hard time concentrating for the rest of the day.

Theodore picked me up from work the way he always did, and we talked about it some more, and then again when we got home. Like he said on the phone, Theodore promised to pay the money back. I did my best to push it out of my mind. Everything was going to be okay.

Theodore did exactly what he said, he paid the money back and I was able to breathe once again -- at least in my marriage. But during this time, I found out that my father was sick.

For months, my father had been having problems with urinating and when he finally went to the doctor, he was told that he was in renal failure. He was taken to a hospital in Salisbury, North Carolina -- Salisbury Memorial -- and at first, I was very concerned. That hospital was known for being extremely prejudice, but when the doctors gave my Dad a machine that he could use at home, I was relieved.

My father was able to use it for a couple of months, but then, one day he passed out and my sister called and told me that our father had been rushed back to Salisbury Memorial.

This time, though, the hospital's racism was in full display. My younger brother called to tell me the news

"They say he's going to die, Evie!" Clarence said.

"What?"

"The doctors said there's nothing they can do. They said he's going to die."

"That's all they said? Just like that?" I couldn't believe what my brother was telling me. It didn't make sense to me. "He's not going to die. What he needs is dialysis. Do they have him seeing a specialist?" I asked. "Is he seeing a nephrologist?"

"I don't know, Ever Lee. I don't know what kind of doctor he's seeing and they didn't say anything about dialysis. They just said there's nothing that they can do for him."

"Well, I need to talk to one of the doctors," I told my brother. "Get one of them to call me. Or get a number where I can call them."

My brother agreed, but the doctors never called. They were not going to talk to me and I knew that they didn't care. If we allowed it, they were just going to let my father die.

I wasn't going to let that happen, though. I knew that all my father needed was treatment. He needed to see a nephrologist, he needed dialysis. But I was in New Jersey and my father was in North Carolina. I wasn't sure what to do, so I called the hospital in Winston Salem and was put through to a doctor.

I told the doctor my name, and everything I could about the situation. "All my father needs is dialysis," I said to the doctor after I told him everything. "I'm sure of that."

The doctor had quietly listened to me, and then after he asked me a few questions, he said, "I'm a nephrologist, and I think you're right."

I had never felt so relieved. I felt as if the doctor had been put there, just waiting for me.

"Okay, this is what we'll do," the doctor began. "Get your father over here to the hospital." He had barely gotten those words out of his mouth before he changed his mind. "No, no, I'll send an ambulance for him."

I gave the doctor all of the information for the hospital and that same day, my father was taken from Salisbury and moved to Winston-Salem. They put him on dialysis and my father was able to live a quality life. I was always so grateful for that doctor.

At home, my life continued with Theodore. I worked full time, while he worked part time. We still spent most of our free time together.

Then another year passed and one day in 1996, I was at work waiting for Theodore to pick me up. I was eager to get home because it was a Thursday and Thursdays were the days when my reader came to our home. Once a week, Stacy, a volunteer came to read and run errands with me. That was something I always looked forward to.

But on this particular day, Theodore didn't show up. It didn't make sense; even if he didn't drive me in the morning to work, he was always the one to pick me up. I began to worry, so I called our next door neighbor.

"Can you go and see if Stacy is already there? And then, can you knock on the door to see if Theodore is still home? He didn't pick me up so maybe he fell asleep or something."

"Okay," my neighbor said. "I'll call you right back.

And when she did, Stacy was on her line. "I've been ringing the doorbell," Stacy said, "and

Theodore is not home. His car isn't even here. But don't worry, I'll come and get you."

So, I stood there, waiting for Stacy and wondering what had happened to my husband. When she arrived, we chatted like there was nothing wrong, but I was very concerned. Theodore not picking me up was something that was out of the ordinary.

When we got to my house, I looked for signs of what might have happened to Theodore. Walking through the living room and the kitchen and den, I saw nothing. There was no sign of Theodore and nothing was out of order. But there was just an air -- I knew that something was wrong.

I went into our bedroom and checked out his closet. I wasn't looking for his clothes. Theodore had a safe where he kept important papers and documents and something told me to check that. When I reached down for his safe, it was gone.

"Oh, my gosh!" I said to myself. "What is going on?"

We had only been married for four years and now, my husband was gone.

When I returned to the living room, Stacy

said, "Maybe we should call the police."

"I was thinking the same thing," I told her. "But it's just been a couple of hours. Even though I know something is wrong, the police won't do anything. At least not yet."

But if I couldn't call the police, I could call everyone else. First, I started with Theodore's doctor. I was thinking that he may have had a medical emergency because recently, he'd started having a twitch under his eye. I didn't even know it until my mother mentioned it and asked me what was wrong.

So I thought of that, and called the doctor to see if he knew anything. But of course, they couldn't give me any information. Then, I called the local hospitals to see if he'd been admitted anywhere.

Finally, I called his best friend who didn't live too far away.

"Bill, have you seen or spoken to Theodore?"

"Yeah, he did come by here earlier today, but I think there was something wrong. He wasn't clear, it was almost like he was incoherent."

"What do you mean?"

"Well, I asked him what was wrong, but if I

didn't know better, I would've thought he'd had a stroke or something."

"Oh, my gosh!"

That news from Bill scared me, but at least now, I could go to the police with something. So, I called the police, told them what I knew and then, they really started searching for him.

The police were not alone. Now, I called my family members and friends, and everyone got involved in the search for Theodore. My friends and family jumped into their cars driving around, looking for him. At first, I wasn't sure if that was going to help or not, but it actually did.

My sister Rosie's daughter, Rosita, actually saw Theodore driving around and she called me back to tell me how she'd pulled up right next to him.

"My car was right next to his, Aunt Evie, and I kept calling him and telling him that you were worried, but he just kept staring forward. He didn't even look at me. And then, he just pulled off. I didn't follow him. I wanted to come home and call you. It was so scary."

I was as afraid as my niece, and for hour after hour, I worried. I didn't sleep at all that night.

Not until I got the call, after five the next morning that Theodore had been found. The police had pulled him over and when they tried to talk to him he was despondent, so they ended up taking him to the hospital. But, I was grateful. At least he'd been found, and now, he was safe.

I contacted Theodore's sister in Philadelphia to let everyone know that he was fine, although he was in the hospital. He stayed in the hospital for a week, but the thing is, I never found out what had happened to him, I never found out what was wrong. Every time I went to the hospital, I just missed the doctor. When I was there in the morning, they told me the doctor had been there last night. When I went at night, they'd told me the doctor had been there in the morning. So, I never had any answers from any medical personnel. The only one who could answer my questions was Theodore and he wasn't giving me any information.

"You don't need to worry, Evie," Theodore told me. "They thought I had a stroke, but I didn't. I'm fine. I just have to follow up with my regular doctor."

I was happy when I was finally able to take

him home, but I still didn't know what to think or believe. Even though I was his wife, I knew nothing. But I couldn't spend my days worrying, so I threw myself into things that would keep me busy. I focused on work, and I got more involved with different organizations, especially the National Federation of the Blind and the National Association of Negro, Business and Professional Women's Clubs, Inc., where I was the Vice-President for the Delaware Valley Chapter.

I kept my focus on these organizations and doing community service. I was awarded Woman of the Year with the National Association of Negro, Business and Professional Women's Clubs and I was the employee of the year for Camden County. In addition to working as much as I could in the community, I traveled back and forth to North Carolina as often as I could to check on my father's health.

Keeping my mind on other things helped me not to think so much about Theodore. It wasn't that I wasn't concerned about him. I was very concerned because he kept going back and forth to the doctor and I could tell that he wasn't well.

I kept asking him, "Theodore, what is going on? What can I do to help?"

"I'm going to be fine." That was all he would say to me and then, as if he were trying to change the subject, he always added, "I'm so proud of you, Evie. You're doing well, you've gained so much confidence in yourself -- you're going to go places, you're going to do big things."

I didn't know if that was just to take the focus off of him, or what. But he would always say things like that to me. So, like I said, I turned my focus onto things that I could control.

But little things just kept happening with Theodore. Like when it was time for me and Theodore to pay our income taxes -- we didn't do it until the very last day. Theodore and I drove over to Philadelphia to mail our income tax payment on April 15th just before midnight.

But as we drove, he was so nervous, he could hardly talk to me. I kept asking him what was wrong, but he wouldn't give me an answer. Something was going on, but I couldn't figure out what it was. For weeks, I'd been telling him that we had to get our tax returns together and had to pay. I never wanted to file at the last minute even though that's what ended up happening.

So at the eleventh hour, we were making that drive. Theodore went inside the Post Office to mail our tax return.

I pushed that out of my mind, though I had no idea that this issue was going to come up again.

And it came up in September of 1996.

Just like before, I was waiting for Theodore to pick me up from work and he never came. Here was Stacy again picking me up again, but there were a couple of things different this time. First of all, the van was in the driveway, Theodore hadn't taken the car. And then, when Stacy and I went into my house, I had that same fearful feeling. This time, though, my husband had left clues.

When I walked into the kitchen, Stacy said, "Take a look at this."

She picked up an envelope and I asked her to read it to me. It was a letter addressed to me from the IRS; they were going to garnish my wages because our taxes had not been paid. Not only for that year, but the taxes hadn't been paid since I'd been with Theodore, not for the years that we'd filed together.

I couldn't believe it. We had just driven to Philadelphia -- what had Theodore done?

Then, next to the letter were the keys to the van.

I already knew that Theodore had left, even before I checked his closet and saw that his best suits were gone. Stacy had followed me upstairs and I told her, "He won't be back this time, he's gone for good."

"No, Evie, don't say that."

"But it's true. He's sick, something else is going on, I don't know. But I know he won't be back."

"Well, did he say anything?"

"No," I told her. "He's being very secretive. I don't know what it is or what's going on. But something is wrong and has been for a long time."

Even though I knew he wasn't coming back, I still made the calls. Of course, I started with Theodore's children. Neither of them had heard from him, nor did they have any idea where he could be.

They all rushed over to my house to comfort

me. And, I had to do a lot of comforting myself because everyone was very emotional. When I told them all what had been going on, the doctor's visits, the secrets, and then, the IRS letter and the van keys, they all agreed with me -- Theodore was not coming back.

"He's sick," someone said.

"But what's wrong with him?"

None of us could really answer that question, though Theodore's children suspected that this could have something to do with Agent Orange. Information was just coming out in the news about that and Theodore had been part of the Armed Services. I didn't know much about his experiences in the army. He never talked much about it, and when he did, he seemed so angry with the army and with the government.

But no matter how long we sat there, talking, we came to the conclusion that there were just no answers. We didn't know a thing.    After everyone left, I thought once again about calling the police. But since Theodore hadn't taken the car, I knew he was long gone...either on a train, or a bus, or a plane. And really, I wasn't so sure that I wanted to find him. Not that I didn't want to know where he was, but even though I'd lived like everything was okay, it had been so stressful with Theodore, knowing that there was something wrong with my husband, but not having any way to find out exactly what it was, and therefore not having any way to help.

I went on with my life, living every day as if things were the same, though nothing was. Once I was sure that Theodore wasn't coming back, I changed the locks, and I even had to have an alarm system put in because I became so fearful. It wasn't that I was afraid of Theodore, but I was afraid that he might come back one day, just appearing in my basement somehow, scaring me to death. F
or the longest time, I walked around my home in fear. And finally, I had to ask God to deliver me from that.

After a while, I did calm down, and my life returned to normal. I went to work, I was active in my organizations -- the only thing that was missing in my life was my husband.

# Chapter 29

It was a difficult time, wondering where Theodore was, wondering why he'd left. I did everything that I could to focus on other things, to keep my life going. Of course, I had the National Federation of the Blind and my other organizations. But then, a major blessing came -- in the form of the television show, "60 Minutes."

Henry Wieneck, a journalist and historian, decided to write a book chronicling the racially intertwined Hairston clan. He wanted to tell the story of the white Hairstons, who were the Rockefellers of slavery, owning over 40 plantations and ten thousand slaves, and the black Hairstons, who were the descendants of those slaves.

It was in 1996 when Henry first told me about the project. And part of the project was going to be a "60 Minutes" interview with many of the Hairstons. Henry told me that CBS wanted me to be part of that program.

"I think your story is very interesting, Ever Lee, and it will add to the piece."

I agreed to do it and in 1997 Henry attended our family reunion, along with CBS to get footage for the television show.

Now, our reunions weren't ordinary family reunions; it was a big business with us. As a family, the Hairstons are incorporated. And at that reunion in 1997, there were over 700 attendees.

How did we become so large and so strong? The Hairston plantation owners very rarely sold their slaves. That philosophy kept the slave families in tact and when slavery ended, over 700 black Hairstons showed up at the clerk's office to register their marriages and list their children for the records.

From the beginning, it was all about family and that was something that my grandfather greatly believed in. He felt it was important for us to know as many of our relatives as possible.

My grandfather also wanted black Hairstons to visit the plantation house and learn the history of the plantation because he often said "Our blood is in this soil." Many of the slaves had helped to build the plantation house.

So the family reunions were a very important part of our lives.

It was exciting to have Henry Wieneck there with us. Especially since this was the year when we'd invited Judge Peter Hairston, one of the white Hairstons, to come to our reunion.

Judge Peter was the son of Miss Elmer when I was growing up on the Cooleemee Plantation. I'd known this man since I was a child. And he knew me. Through the years, we'd had a good relationship. Even when I left, even when my parents moved away, I would go back and visit the plantation occasionally and see Judge Peter.

I always spoke at the reunions and that year was no different. But this time, when I went up to the stage, I decided to speak about something that I had never said publicly. With Judge Peter sitting there, I put a voice to the feelings I'd had for years. From the time I was a child on that plantation, I'd resented the way the black Hairstons were treated. And at that reunion, I told Judge Peter that. In front of the one thousand attendees, I called him out. I told the judge that he and his family had mistreated my family.

"My parents and grandparents worked their heads off for your family and for very little money!"

At first, a hush came over the room. I'd shocked everyone. But I wasn't sorry for what I'd said. I'd held those feelings and thoughts inside for so long, it was time for those feelings to come out.

After those few moments of silence, everyone began to clap and then, the room filled with applause. I guess I wasn't the only black Hairston who felt that way. And CBS and Henry Wieneck were there to film it.

In 1998, CBS and Henry came to my home to film parts of my life. They followed me while I went about my day, and then, they even took the trip with me to Washington, DC, where with the National Federation of the Blind, I was on Capitol Hill marching the halls and discussing some of the issues confronting blind people. I was also seeking sponsors and cosponsors for Bills in the House of Representatives and in the Senate for legislation for blind Americans.

The "60 Minutes" segment finally aired in

1999 and not only did the show cover the reunion, but it showed my meeting with Judge Peter afterward when I returned to the plantation. Of course, Judge Peter disagreed with me and what I'd said at the reunion.

"I was the one who ended sharecropping on our land, Ever Lee," he reminded me.

That was true, but it didn't make up for all that my family had gone through. Whether we liked it or not, the black and white Hairstons shared the worst possible event in American history. But at least, we all survived.

That "60 Minutes" program really kept me distracted. And it was after that program aired, that I finally filed for divorce from Theodore.

But before I did, I found out where Theodore was living. Through some personal connections, I discovered that he was living in St. Louis. When I learned that, I gave my information to my attorney to proceed. A few months later, I received my divorce.

I continued to fill my time with my activities in the various organizations to which I belonged. And, I spent as much time as I could with my family in North Carolina.

My father had lived a good life, even though he was on dialysis, but in March of 2000 he was diagnosed with cancer. Just like when my dad had been diagnosed with renal failure, I flew down and spoke with his doctors. His prognosis was like the last time.

"I'm sorry, but your father is in the last stages of stomach cancer. He doesn't have six months to live."

This time, I believed the doctors. My father had been a smoker for years and he chewed tobacco. Many people think those activities lead to lung cancer alone, but they were causes for stomach cancer as well.

For the next six months, my father was in and out of the hospital, progressively getting worse. And in September, we put him in a hospice for the final stages. One day later, he passed away.

Of course, it was a sad occasion, but we had been prepared. And all of us agreed that my father had lived quite a life. He'd been born and raised on the Cooleemee Plantation, and then raised his own children there. Once we were all gone, my mother and father had finally left the plantation, building their own home nearby. He'd had to bury two of his children, but he'd seen the others grow up and do well. My father had lived a good life. And we were all able to celebrate his homegoing.

After my father's funeral, I returned to New Jersey and about a year later, I finally had news about Theodore. I received a call from his daughter.

"Evie, I have some news about dad. I just got a call from the V.A.," she said, sounding very upset. "Dad is coming home. He's being sent from St. Louis to the V.A. hospital here in Philadelphia because he's dying of cancer."

She went on to tell me that Theodore had bone cancer, and they weren't giving him a good prognosis. They didn't think that he would survive very long.

When I hung up from her, I didn't know what I was feeling. The way Theodore had left caused a lot of mixed feelings, all the secrets he'd kept, I just didn't know what was best. At first, I wasn't going to go to see him, but then, I decided that I needed to go to that hospital and see Theodore. I needed this closure because he had just walked out of my life and had never looked back. I needed to understand why. But there was no way that I wanted to go by myself and my best friend, Judy, agreed to take me to see him.

When Judy and I got to the hospital, of course, I couldn't see him, but I could hear him. And he sounded much different. Much weaker. But it seemed like Theodore was glad to see me.

"Evie, I saw you on TV. I saw you on '60 Minutes.' I told you that I was proud of you and that you were going to be doing big things."

But I didn't want to talk about that. I asked, "Theodore, why did you leave?"

"It was all best for you, Evie."

"But I was so hurt, Theodore. I was so, so hurt, and I just don't understand." When he didn't say anything, I added, "But I want you to know that I came her to tell you that I've forgiven you for your selfish behavior."

I don't know if he planned to say anything else. At that moment, his brother and sister-in-law came into the room. I hugged both of them and then I said goodbye to Theodore before Judy and I left.

Two days later, I received the call from his

daughter. It was a sad time, but I had made my closure with Theodore.

Yes, I had forgiven him, but I had not forgotten. It was still so hard for me to reconcile how he'd walked out on me, without any explanation and leaving me wondering. I didn't deserve that kind of treatment from him.

Even though his family contacted me and gave me all the information for the funeral, I didn't go. I couldn't go. I couldn't put myself through people coming up to me and giving me their condolences when I had not seen or been with Theodore for five years.

I was no longer his wife, I didn't need to be there. I already had my closure.

# Chapter 30

The Christmas after Theodore died, I went to Illinois to spend the holidays with my son, Victor and his girlfriend, Brenda.

Victor had been living in California and over the years, I'd spent a lot of time in Santa Barbara and Los Angeles with him just visiting and celebrating the holidays. I'd had the chance to meet Brenda and I really liked her. So, I was delighted when Brenda invited me to go to Illinois to celebrate the holidays with her family.

My son's girlfriend is Caucasian and my friends and I kidded about my trip being a real life "Guess Who's Coming to Dinner."

Of course, it was anything but that. There was no tension at all; Brenda and her family welcomed me with open arms. They treated me as if I was already part of the family; I had a great time.

I thought Victor had wanted me there in Illinois because we spent most holidays together.

But I had no idea what he was up to until the evening when Victor presented Brenda with an engagement ring.

When my son said to Brenda, "Will you marry me?" I jumped up and marched around the room seven times. "Thank God, thank God, thank God!" I shouted.

I was so happy because I truly believed that the union between Victor and Brenda was a marriage that had been put together by God.

From that point until June, 2002, I spent all of my time thinking about and helping them prepare for the wedding. While I helped them with the things they had to get done, there were a few personal things I wanted to do in time for their wedding as well.

For my son's wedding, I decided that I was going to be a new Evie. This was a new day, my son was entering into a new part of his life, So, I wanted to celebrate their day by being the very best that I could be, too.

I'd even decided to have an escort at their wedding. I'd been dating Mark for about fourteen months. I'd met him at church and we'd gone out a few times. We did lots of things together: going out to dinner and jazz concerts. We went to New York to catch a couple of plays a few times. And of course, we attended church events together. But even though I enjoyed our outings, I knew, though, that Mark and I would not be in a relationship for very long. I discovered early that he was a very jealous and possessive man. He always wanted to know where I was, where I was going, who I was with.

But I thought it would be a good idea to have him go with me to California to the wedding. Now, I knew when I made that decision, some might say that was bad judgment on my part because I'd already seen how jealous he could be. But, I really wanted Mark with me because I didn't want Victor or Brenda to be spending their time feeling responsible for me. I knew they would be concerned all the time, thinking, "Is Mom okay?" and I didn't want that. Especially not on their big day. The focus had to be all on them.

Honestly, I didn't think Mark could do anything at the wedding, and if he did, I was just going to ignore him. There was no way I was going to allow him to mess up that wonderful time for me and my son.

So, in June of 2002, I went to California with Mark and two of my best friends, Judy and Rosemary. Of course, one of the first things that happened was that Mark became jealous. And it was ridiculous because he was jealous of Victor and the time I was spending with my son. Mark wanted me to be at the hotel with him.

But like I promised myself, I ignored him; I was just there to celebrate my son's marriage. The wedding was beautiful, held in a unique church in Santa Barbara, with one side of the church all glass, overlooking the mountain.

Judy's daughter, Michelle, sang and Judy accompanied her. Brenda's brother in-law and my brother, Clarence conducted the ceremony. The reception was wonderful and I even had a good time there with Mark. He'd always been an excellent dancer and so while we were there, we had a good time. I knew though, that Mark was not the man for me because he couldn't wait until we returned to New Jersey before demonstrating his jealousy in a very controlling manner. So when I returned to New Jersey, that was the end of my relationship with Mark.

But my life went on with my focus on my job and the Federation.

I'd been working for the agency since 1983, and though I was confident and was blessed to be doing well, I was getting worn out, stressed out, and burned out. But even with all of that, I was really moving up.

Right before Victor's wedding, I'd been promoted to become the Director for the Intoxicated Drivers Resource Center in Sedona, New Jersey. I was thrilled about my new position because I was going to be able to make even more of a difference. When I think about how I had walked into the agency and started at the very bottom, I knew this was an accomplishment. And though it had taken many years, I'd made it to the top. I was the only blind person working in the agency at that time and I had been a supervisor for many years. Now, I was the director.

Even though that was such a good time, such a great promotion, there was some sadness surrounding that. Although I had moved up, was performing quite well, and had major accomplishments for the agency (like getting a grant and helping the agency keep its license with New Jersey,) I still wasn't being paid the salary of the other sighted workers. (And that is something that the National Federation of the Blind is still fighting for today). Fair Wages For Workers With Disability.

In spite of all of that, I was committed to my job. I fulfilled my responsibilities because of the training, philosophy, and skills that I'd learned at the Louisiana Center for the Blind. By mastering the alternative skills that I'd been taught, I was able to compete with my colleagues. It meant a lot to me to be able to show everyone that a blind employee could perform just as well as a sighted one and be successful.

And succeed, I did.

# Chapter 31

While my career was going well, my personal life was moving along, too.

First...I became a grandmother! Victor and Brenda had a baby! My first grandchild, Kendall. And the best part -- I was there in California when he was born.

I flew to Los Angeles for the impending birth, and three days later, Brenda went into labor. I went with them to the hospital because both Victor and Brenda welcomed me there to witness the delivery. That was such a wonderful, amazing time that I will always cherish.

Once I returned home, I started dating again.

I attended the NFB convention in Maryland and was even more excited about this one than the other ones because I'd been asked to do a seminar for blind teenagers. But of course, I attended all the other seminars, too.

On one of the first days at the convention, I entered into one of the auditoriums and as I was walking down the aisle, using my cane, I kept asking those who were already there, "Is this seat taken? Is this seat taken?" I was looking for an aisle seat.

Finally, a gentleman told me that there was a seat next to him. When I sat down, he introduced himself to me and then, Henry asked, "Did you come in here by yourself?"

"Yes, of course," I said, not quite understanding the question.

"How did you do that?"

I said, "Using my cane." In my mind, I wanted to ask him how else did he expect me to get around?

He said, "Well, I want to get to the restaurant afterward. Would you mind showing me how to navigate this hotel?"

"Sure. When this is over, I'll show you how we do it." I sensed from his questions, that he didn't have the confidence to move around by himself. I understood that. Before I'd gone to the Center, sometimes, I felt the same way. So, I told him, "Maybe you should go to one of the centers and get some training."

He didn't respond to that, but we sat through

the rest of the seminar, and then as promised, I showed him around the hotel. Then, we went to the restaurant and he treated me to lunch. We chatted about the Federation and I told him how much the networking and the Center had helped me.

Afterward, I thanked him, told him that maybe I would see him at the banquet later that night, and then, I went on to my own seminar.

Now there were always so many people at our conventions, that I didn't have any expectation of seeing Henry again. But when I went into the banquet hall that night, he was seated right next to me!

I couldn't believe it. What were the chances of that? And that's what I told him. "Out of all of these tables, how did we end up together?"

He said, "I arranged it."

It turned out that Henry had told the people who were assigning everyone to their tables that he wanted to sit with Ever Hairston because, "She was quite helpful to me today." And so they'd put us together.

That was the beginning of Henry and I dating. He lived in Greenbelt, Maryland and he would come to New Jersey to visit me and we talked often on the phone. Henry was what's called high partial; he could really see quite well, at first. But he was slowly losing his vision. And as he went through that process, he became more and more depressed. He really felt sorry for himself and worried about what his life was going to be like.

I tried to encourage him to get help. I told him the difference that the Center had made for me. Finally, I talked him into going to the agency in Baltimore.

But even after some training and learning alternative skills, he had difficulty accepting his blindness.

I felt Henry moving more and more toward depression, feeling sorry for himself. The more I encouraged him to network and get involved, the more he withdrew. He just had no more confidence in himself. And he got further into his own shell.

As Henry withdrew, I was going out even more. His confidence was getting lower and mine was building. I told him that I saw us drifting apart and we stopped dating.

But that was not the only part of my life that was changing, or coming to an end, so to speak. In 2006, after being with the agency for twenty-six years, and working my way up to the director, I retired.

It was my decision. The agency was already beginning to downsize and they were closing several departments. I just felt like that was a great time for me to leave because there were some decisions I had to make about my life.

The year before, Victor and Brenda had built a wonderful home in Los Angeles. When I'd gone to visit and they'd given me a tour, I saw the apartment that was part of their house, and I thought they'd added that for tenants.

But then, a few months after I'd helped them move into their home and returned to New Jersey, Victor called and said, "Mom, I think you should consider moving here. You could move into the apartment that's attached to our house."

It took me a moment, but all I could say was, "Huh?"

Then, Brenda added, "Mom, it would be great."

So, now I knew that this wasn't just Victor's

idea. Victor and Brenda both agreed on the idea of me moving there. But, I didn't know about me leaving my life and my friends. Plus, I would have to leave my house in New Jersey.

But the two of them didn't stop. A few months later, Victor called again and said, "Mom, I think it would be to your advantage financially to move here. Now, I know you love your home in Cherry Hill, but that house is going to require maintenance, plus the property taxes are astronomical and you're doing it all by yourself. I just don't think there's any need for you to do that anymore."

Then, he called me a little while later and gave me a new argument, "Mom, remember how you got that house. Maybe it's time for you to pass it on to someone else who needs it."

I knew that Victor was right in so many ways. Especially since that house was too big for me; it really was more than I needed. But, I just didn't want to give it up. I had too many wonderful memories there.

But at the same time, moving to Los Angeles would be a new beginning. It would be like starting all again, but that could be both good and bad.

It was so hard for me to make up my mind. So, I decided to just give this to God. I knew He'd let me know the best decision to make. And that's what I did -- every night, in my prayers I told God that I just didn't know what to do, that this was a tough decision, and I needed His help.

It didn't take long for me to get my answer. It was early one April morning. I woke up and the answer was so clear to me.

I heard that small voice of God say, "Sell your house. It's time to go. It's time to move on."

That voice, that feeling was so strong and so real, that once I heard it, I knew that there was nothing to fear. I didn't have to be afraid of a new life. And the more I thought about it, I felt like I owed it to Victor and Brenda, but I was especially thinking about my grandson, Kendall. My son had never been close to my parents nor his father's parents. I wanted that to be different for my grandchildren.

So, at my job, they were offering those of us who'd been there for twenty-five years a package to retire and I decided to take it. I was going to begin a new life in California.

The first thing on the agenda was to sell my house and it was so interesting the way that happened. I had been sure that God was in the middle of all of this for me, but I was absolutely sure with the sale of my house.

Although Sherlock and I had divorced many years before, I was still friendly with his family. Whenever there was a big family function, Judy and I were invited. Over the years, we'd always wanted our children to stay connected with their fathers' families. So this year, I was invited to the Houston family picnic.

I didn't always go to the functions, but this particular year I felt compelled to go. Especially since Sherlock's father was very ill and I wanted to see him.

At the picnic, I met the woman who was Sherlock's father's caretaker, Mary, and we really connected. The next week, I decided to go to the nursing home to visit Mr. Houston. I wanted to see him in his final days by myself.

When I got there, Mr. Houston was so glad to see me. "Thank you so much for coming, Evie. You know, you are my daughter-in-law. I have a picture of you with the family just like I have pictures of everyone else."

I thanked him for that and told him about my plans to move to California.

"You gonna sell your house?" Mr. Houston asked me.

"Yes, I think it's time."

That was when Mary joined the conversation. "I've been looking for a house."

"Well, I'll let you know when I put my home up for sale."

Mr. Houston passed away soon after that, but over the next few months, Mary and I stayed in touch. And when I finally put my house up for sale, in two months it was gone. Mary was able to purchase it!

I was thrilled about it. From what I knew about Mary, she'd worked hard all her life. Like Victor said, it was someone else's turn; it was Mary's turn to have that house.

But not only that -- I began to think about everything that I had in that house. I loved it all, and there were so many memories, both good and bad. But...did I really want to pack it all up and move it to California? Everything I had, I loved. But it was all material things.

So, in the July, 2006, I sold just about everything in that house -- the living room furniture, all of my kitchen appliances, and the dining room to Mary and her family.

And then, I moved out to Los Angeles. That was July 20, 2006.

# Chapter 32

I was changing my life. Moving from the East Coast to the West.

My brother drove me across the country with my clothes, and the few things that I took from my house, like my dishes, my elephant collection, and knick-knacks.

Once I moved to Los Angeles, I had to furnish the one-bedroom apartment. It wasn't difficult. I needed a bedroom set, of course. And then, something to fill the Great Room.

Brenda and I shopped together, going to the wonderful shops in West Los Angeles where I was able to find the wooden, rustic kind of pieces that I was looking for. This was so different than how I lived in New Jersey, with a lot of modern glass furniture.

But I was starting over here, living a new life. I wanted everything to be different, down to my mattress and the pots and pans in the kitchen.

It was a great time of getting acclimated to California and living with my son and his family.

At the same time, I got more involved with The National Federation of the Blind of California. Now, I was living a very good life.

Then in February, 2008, my life changed again!

My son, Victor, was given an employment opportunity to transfer to Northville, Michigan. It seemed that he had a very secure position in Los Angeles and it was a great position. I thought our lives were going to go on like this forever.

Then one day, Victor came home and said to me and Brenda, "We need to talk." He turned to me and asked, "Mom, are you available after dinner tonight?" Before I could even answer, he said, "Why don't you just have dinner with us? Then, after dinner, we can put the kids to bed and we can talk."

The entire time we were eating, I wondered what Victor could possibly want. But he didn't seem too upset, so I wasn't worried.

After dinner, once the children were put to bed, Brenda and I sat down with great anticipation. What could Victor's news be?

We kept asking him, "Victor, what is it?"

"I'm gonna tell you. Just relax." After we

were settled in the living room, he said, "It looks like I'm going to have to relocate. We're moving to Michigan."

Brenda and I sat there in shock, so that gave Victor time to continue.

He said, "Now, we can do a couple of things. If we decide that we don't want to do this, I can leave my current company, but right now, it would be starting over and I really think this would be a great opportunity for me to advance. I think we have to make this move." My son turned to me and said, "And Mom, I know this is a shock and you haven't been here that long, but I'd love for you to go with us. You're part of this family and if we go, you go."

The tears were streaming down Brenda's face and Victor sat down next to her.

"Honey, are you okay?"

She nodded. "Well, in Michigan, we'll be closer to Mom and Dad," she said about her parents, trying to be optimistic at the same time.

"Victor, I made a big move to be here. So whatever I have to do, I'm here with you." Then, I said, "Let's pray," and led my son and daughter-in-law in prayer.

When I finished, Victor stood and hugged me. "Thank you."

So, we were on our way to Michigan.

The move wasn't very difficult. Again, you can always tell when God is in the middle of something because He will truly work it out.

We moved to Northville, Michigan and stayed in a Residence Inn. Brenda's parents came along as well to help us all get settled.

During the day, Victor and Brenda would go out and look at houses and if they found one that they liked, they'd come back and we'd all go. We all took a look at a couple of houses together, but none that we all agreed on.

One afternoon, while Brenda and Victor were out, their realtor told Victor about a man that Victor just happened to know who was selling his house. Instead of going through the realtor, Victor called him and he and Brenda went over to see his friend.

Well, the two couples sat down and talked and they decided that they would house swap since the other couple was going to California to work with the California affiliate of Victor's company. We moved into their home and they moved into ours.

So, in February of 2008, we moved to Michigan in the middle of one of the worst winters they'd had. We got there in February and we didn't see our deck until sometime in May or June. That's how cold it was and how much it snowed that year.

But, it was a very nice house. I didn't have my own apartment like I did in Los Angeles, but I had my own room and bathroom.

The good thing about being in Michigan was now I got involved with the National Federation of the Blind in Michigan, so I was getting exposure and leadership skills in different affiliates in the United States.

We made it through, though. It wasn't long before Victor was transferred back to California. Just 18 months later, in August of 2009, we went home! Victor was given more responsibilities, and very pleased with his career.

I was happy for Victor and proud of his accomplishments, but I have to admit, I was just as happy to leave that winter in Michigan behind.

# Chapter 33

It was good to be back to the more moderate temperatures of Southern California. This move back to Los Angeles was much more difficult. The family who was in our home relocated to another residence in Los Angeles.

Unpacking, labeling herbs and spices, and other things in Braille took time to organize. The furniture took longer than expected to arrive from Michigan to Los Angeles. So for a while I was without my television and my computer. On top of that, my cell phone wasn't working well. Prior to leaving for Michigan, my cell phone worked fine up in these hills, but on our return, we discovered that the cell towers had been changed and now the signals were not good as before. It was difficult to make and receive calls. Even my landline wasn't working. I felt isolated and couldn't communicate with anyone in the outside world.

Of course, Victor was concerned about me

and my comfort, so one day, he decided that he was going to try to fix my landline himself. After taking a look at the telephone connection in my room, he headed to the garage to get some tools.

"I'll be right back, Mom."

"Okay," I told him, trying not to feel frustrated about it all.

I was standing at the side of my bed, just wishing everything could get back to the way it was, and all of a sudden, my world began to spin. I have no idea what happened. In an instant, everything -- my head, my body, the room, it was all spinning. I grabbed the armoire to the side of my bed, trying to hold myself up. But it was difficult because I was spinning so fast, I couldn't get my bearings. After a couple of moments, I couldn't even hold on anymore. I lost my balance and collapsed onto the floor.

It was just a couple of minutes before Victor returned. But when he saw me, he rushed to my side. "Mom, mom, are you okay?" he asked, as he hit my arm, trying to see if I would respond.

I tried to talk, but I could tell that my speech was slurred and inside, I knew exactly what Victor was thinking -- that I'd had a stroke.

He kept talking to me and though I wanted to respond, I couldn't get too much out, I couldn't really say anything.

"Brenda!" he yelled out to his wife.

The way he screamed, I knew Brenda was going to be down there in a couple of seconds -- which she was.

"Oh, my gosh!" she said. "What's happened?"

"I don't know, but we've got to get help."

"Okay, I'll be right back."

I could hear everything they were saying and I understood what Brenda was going to do. Our neighbor, across the street was a nurse, and I knew Brenda was going to get her. So, my hearing and comprehension was fine; I just couldn't speak.

Of course, Victor didn't leave my side. Just a few minutes later, Brenda rushed back in with our neighbor.

"What's wrong?" she asked Victor as she immediately dropped to the floor next to me.

"I don't know," he said. "She was fine when I stepped out of the room, but when I came back, I found her this way."

Our neighbor went to work. "Can you move

your arm?" she asked me. "Try to move your arm."

I couldn't.

Then, Victor said, "It looks like her face is twisted!"

I wanted to scream; my face was not twisted, and I needed to tell him that. But it was so bizarre. I could hear, I could understand, I just couldn't speak.

Minutes later, the EMTs came and took over. They took my vital signs and then together, lifted me onto the gurney and took me out to the ambulance. Not too long after that, I was admitted into Cedar Sinai Hospital.

That was when all the testing started. First in the Emergency Room and then in my own room. Slowly, my speech came back to me and I was able to move, but they kept me in the hospital as they did everything from MRIs to all other kinds of scans and blood tests to see if I'd had a stroke. Two days later, they were pretty sure that I hadn't had a stroke, but the doctors wondered if I had a TIA -- Trans Iscemic Attack, which is a mini-stroke where the symptoms don't last very long But then, they ruled that out.

A few days later, a neurologist came to tell me that they'd figured it out. He explained to me that I had a blockage behind my right eye.

"Wow! How did that happen?"

"Well, there could be a number of factors, stress, and then your cholesterol levels are high."

I didn't understand how this had happened. The entire time I was in Michigan, I was working out. Believe me, there was little else to do, especially in the middle of winter. So, I went to a fitness club regularly. Besides, church and visiting with a few friends occasionally, that's all I did.

"Okay," I said, "so what are you going to do?"

"Well, I'm afraid that if we try to remove it, you'll have a stroke." He explained to me that with an operation, the blockage could move and go to my brain. "We're going to look into a couple of things, maybe medication and other options. Give us a few days and we'll figure this out."

I ended up staying in the hospital for a week, and after they put me on medication, I left the hospital with instructions to see a neurologist regularly.

Of course, I was going to follow the doctor's instructions, but at the same time, I took my desire to be healed to God. I started praying, "Lord, I'm not claiming this, I don't want this. This must not be."

I prayed that prayer all the time, all the while taking my medication and going to the doctor. There were lifestyle changes that I made as well -- I kept exercising and I made sure that I was eating a healthy, balanced diet, which was something that I tried to do all the time anyway. Of course, I kept my appointments with the neurologist, too.

Three months later, the doctor scheduled an appointment so that I could have another MRI as well as several other tests. I had to stay in the hospital for a few days, and when the doctor came into my room to go over the results, at first, I thought something wasn't right. I could hear the puzzlement in his voice.

"What's wrong?" I asked.

He spoke slowly. "Nothing. I don't know what you're doing, but we cannot find the blockage. No blockage can be found at all!"

I knew what I was doing, but I didn't say

anything to him.

The doctor said, "Whatever you're doing, just keep doing it."

He didn't have to tell me that. I knew; I was always going to keep on praying.

So, I walked out of the hospital with the blockage gone and I was healthy, once again. But that experience was a great teaching experience for me. Because it was then when I realized that no matter what was going on in my life, I had to make the best of each day. I was determined that from that point on, I was going to live my life to the fullest. I wasn't going to allow myself to be stressed over minor things, especially not over things that I couldn't change, but always felt that it was necessary to accept the things I cannot change, but to have the courage to change the things I can. Every day, I was just going to keep moving forward.

From that point, that's what I did. All I can say is what a difference that attitude made. Even when I had to return to the hospital six months later for vertigo, which is extreme dizziness, I kept my attitude. And just like before, it turned out that I was just fine.

# Chapter 34

That next Christmas, I went to North Carolina to celebrate the holidays with my mother.

And I really got involved extensively with the National Federation of the Blind of California. I'd always been part of the Affiliate, but now, I was given the responsibility of Membership Developer for California. I also spoke at events on our Affiliate's behalf, and I served on quite a few committees.

I was elected as Second Vice President of the National Federation of the Blind of California and I got more involved at the National level, serving on many committees. Therefore I had to spend more time at our National Headquarters in Baltimore, MD.

Personally, I took it up a notch, too. I went back to the Braille Institute to brush up on my computer skills, take Internet courses, and to take a refresher course in Braille.

I did all of that, just opening up my life to experience more. And, it's interesting what happens when you do that because my life changed, especially with my responsibilities with the Federation.

I arrived at the 2010 convention in Dallas, Texas a day early, which is something that I always did. I'd only been checked in a few minutes when I received a call from our National president, Dr. Marc Maurer, the President of the Federation.

Dr. Maurer said, "Ever Lee, do you have some time? I'd like you to come to the presidential suite. I'd like to talk to you."

"Okay," I said. "Just give me a few minutes and I'll be there."

But the moment I hung up, I asked myself what in the world could Dr. Maurer want with me. I couldn't imagine, but I wanted to find out.

So, I changed out of my traveling clothes and then made my way to Dr. Maurer's suite. When I got there, one of the board members was at the front desk in his suite.

"Oh, Ever Lee, Dr. Maurer is waiting on you." And then, she directed me inside.

The minute I walked in, Dr. Maurer told me to have a seat. Then, he got right to the point.

"Ever Lee," he began, "do you know the responsibilities of a board member?"

"I think I do."

"Well, what do you think?"

"I think one of the greatest responsibilities of a board member is to support the president."

"That's right," he said, as if I'd just gotten the answer right on a test. "Ever Lee, you've been part of this Federation for a long time and I can see that you're a very committed member. You're really liked and respected and you know how to inspire and motivate people."

"Thank you," I said, not knowing where he was going with this.

"Well, if you are nominated to serve on the National Board would you accept?"

That was a shocker to me. "Me? Oh, my goodness." One of the reasons I was so surprised was I thought national board members were appointed after being State presidents. And that's what I told Dr. Maurer.

"Yes, that's how it was at one time. And even now, some people would think that, but there are changes being made with the board, and there's always an exception to the rule. And anyway, I would like to see you on the board."

Dr. Maurer went on to explain that it would be for one term and that I'd be replacing the board member who was the State president of Georgia, but who had to resign from the board because he'd accepted a position at the National Center in Baltimore, MD.

At first, I didn't know what to say.

"Do you think this is gonna be a problem for Mary?" Dr. Maurer asked, referring to Mary Willows, the president of the National Federation of the Blind of California.

"I don't know," I answered. "I don't think so, but I can't speak for her."

"Has she arrived yet?"

"No, she's coming in this afternoon."

"Well, when she gets in, let her know that I'd like to speak to the two of you."

"Okay," I said, getting up to leave. All the way back to my room, I thought about what Dr. Maurer had told me and while I was surprised, I was also honored. The more I thought about it, the more I realized that being on the board was really something that I wanted to do. Being on the board would give me additional and welcomed responsibilities.

When Mary arrived a few hours later, I called to tell her about the conversation I'd had with Dr. Maurer.

"He wants to nominate me for the board, Mary. And I'd like to know what you think about that?"

"I think it's great," she said.

Even though she spoke positively, I kinda detected just a little bit of apprehension. I was beginning to think that this wasn't going to be as easy as I thought. But then, she added, "Really, Evie, it's all right with me, but I think Robert and some of the others are not going to be too happy."

Robert was the Second Vice President of the National Federation of the Blind - California.

"Okay, well, Dr. Maurer would like to speak to both of us."

An hour later, we were both sitting in front of him and Dr. Maurer repeated the conversation he'd had with me. He told Mary, "Ever Lee has lived in many places and I think she'll bring a unique perspective to the board. She's been committed to the Federation and that's why I want to nominate her." He paused. "Do you have any objections to that?"

"No," Mary said.

Dr. Maurer said, "That's exactly what I wanted to hear. Because California needs Ever Lee and I think she's a great asset there in California. I wouldn't want any animosity as a result of this nomination."

"No," Mary said again. "I think you're right about Ever Lee."

So, that was it. Mary was very supportive of me and Dr. Maurer's desire to have me on the board. Over the next few days, the word was buzzing around the convention that I was going to be nominated to be on the board. As each day passed, though, I got more and more nervous. All of the talk, all of the buzz, all of the excitement, it was a lot.

But three days later, just like Dr. Maurer said, he announced to the entire convention, "The board has placed Ever Lee Hairston's name as a nomination for the board of the National Federation for the Blind."

When they asked if there were any other nominations, none came from that floor and that's when Dr. Maurer called out to me.

"Ever Lee! We need to hear from you!"

I wasn't expecting that. I didn't know that I was going to have to speak, but I'd done this before and I was so excited to address the convention. I went up on the stage, stood at the microphone.

"First, I want to thank everyone for their confidence in me. I fought the fight for civil rights in the 60's under the leadership of Dr. Martin Luther King, Jr. and here, I will have the opportunity to do it again for the Federation. I've been doing that for years, but now, I won't just be a member, I'll be a member of the board. I promise that I will work very hard to advocate for our rights for the blind. And so any one of you who choose not to get on this bandwagon with me...."

Everyone laughed and stood to their feet, applauding, giving me a standing ovation.

I was so happy; everyone was excited for me. Not only did everyone know that I was going to work hard and do a good job, but much of the excitement was because I was black. I was going to be the first black female elected to the board.

And so, in July, 2010, at that convention, I was elected to be one of the seventeen members of the board for the National Federation of the Blind.

And right away, I hit the ground running. I'd always been committed to the Federation, but with this new position, I was given responsibilities that kept me busy and traveling. I was under the impression that a new board member would serve a few years before being assigned to represent the president at state conventions. But it wasn't that way for me. I was given that responsibility from the very beginning. I have served as the national representative at many of the State conventions.

My very first time was in Tennessee, and since that time, I have been all over the United States.

As a National Rep, I'm responsible for giving the report from the National office. My responsibilities as a Board member at the state conventions are to fill the state in on all of our programs that are going on at the national office, and I speak about the upcoming national convention. The whole idea when I go to a state convention is to get the people on the state level involved. To inform them about our programs, projects, resources and how they can make contributions to further build a future of possibilities for the Blind.

But my responsibilities went beyond attending the state conventions. As a board member, I am an advocate for the National Federation of the Blind and make presentations to Congress to affect government policy. I work with other Board members to get sponsors in the Senate and in the House for bills that affect the blind. And then, I keep our membership up to date with reports on the status of the issues we have before Congress. We also do a special outreach to Veterans and have a program called, Early Explorers, which provides resources to enable young blind children to travel independently. We help children understand the importance of using a cane as a travel tool before they've even perfected the ability to walk. There are a number of other programs including a Braille Enrichment program for literacy and learning, and a special education program that serves fifty blind high school students from across the country. That program is held at Towson University each year in late July.

I especially like speaking about the training Centers that we have and then, I enjoy speaking to the special groups -- like Seniors, or teens. Often, I'm the keynote speaker for their luncheons.

My responsibilities wrap up at the banquet on the last evening of each convention. Serving on the Board and fulfilling all of duties has been a pleasure for me and since I started with the Board, I do about six conventions throughout the year.

In 2011, I had to be re-elected since my term was just to replace another Board member. So, I had to speak once again, and once again, I was elected.

While we got a lot of work done at the conventions, it was also a great time for us to socialize and catch up. Aleceae, a friend of mine, always got a suite and a group of us would hang out, catch up on everything that had happened to us through the year, chat and tell jokes. That year, though, all of my friends wanted to just celebrate my election to the Board. They were all just so excited about me being on the Board and they talked about how I was a role model and inspiration.

I felt good that I could do that for them. I really wanted everyone to be the best that they could be and not feel in any way limited by their blindness.

I had no idea, though, that my inspiration would introduce me to a new friend...a new person in my life.

# Chapter 35

In November 2011, I was assigned as the national representative for the National Federation of the Blind -- New Jersey. I was thrilled to be returning to the state where I really got started with the Federation.

It was exciting to be returning "home" and the moment I landed in Newark Airport, I received an email from Ponchie, a friend who I'd met at the various conventions. He was part of the group who hung out in Alecea's suite, and so I knew him, though not very well.

His email said that he was going to be in New Jersey, too, which was interesting since he lived out West. But he wrote that he hoped we'd be able to get together for lunch or dinner.

"I know national reps are usually really busy," his email said. "So, I hope you'll be able to find the time."

I thought that would be nice, but I knew my schedule in New Jersey was going to be intense. From the time I landed, the folks in New Jersey had me going. The president of the New Jersey chapter had a radio interview scheduled, he had me speaking to the parents...I went from one thing to the next. That entire first day, that Friday, I felt like I was on roller skates. I never got a chance to even email Ponchie back.

Finally on Friday evening, there was a talent show and I had a chance to step outside and sit out in the lobby of the hotel. That was the first chance I had to email Ponchie and tell him that I was at the talent show. I asked where he was and then told him that I would be free the next day around lunch time.

He wrote me right back and said that would be great and we made arrangements to meet at the dining room.

But between the time when I sent the message to Ponchie and lunch the next day, my calendar filled up. So, I didn't have time for a long lunch.

"I'm really sorry," I told Ponchie when we met up. "I think I'll only have time for soup." I told him how Bob had me running.

"Boy, they really keep you guys busy."

"It's just the president. I'm not this busy

everywhere I go."

He laughed, but then became serious, "Evie, you know how proud we all are of you, right?"

"Thanks," I said, already knowing that. That was one of the reasons that I wanted to do my job well. But then, I just had to add, "But this is a lot of work."

We both laughed about that.

"Look, maybe you can have a drink after the banquet speech tonight."

"That's a deal," I said, glad that he was so understanding of my time.

So after that quick lunch, I dashed away and every hour of my day was filled all the way up to the banquet.

The banquet was always the highlight of the convention where we dressed up and wrapped up the events of the two days. This convention was extra special for me. My nephew, Rosie's son who lived there in New Jersey, came out to the banquet to see and support me. It had been a while since I'd seen him and I was glad to have him there.

And Buddy was glad to be there, too. When the banquet was over, he came to me. "Aunt

Evie, you were so good. It was wonderful."

He'd not heard me speak except at family reunions. I thanked him for coming. I hugged him and said, "It was so nice to have you here, Larry."

Then, I felt a tap on my shoulder. "I'm here, too," I heard Ponchie say.

"Oh, how are you?" I turned and introduced Ponchie to Larry.

After they exchanged hellos, Ponchie whispered, "There's a long line of people waiting to speak to you."

"Yeah, Aunt Evie," Larry said. "You're gonna be here for a long time talking to everyone, so, I'm gonna get out of here." He kissed me on the cheek. "I'll see you later."

When Larry left, Ponchie kinda stepped to the side, too, as I greeted everyone who came up to me to thank me for my speech.

"It was so motivating."

"You inspire me!"

"We're so proud of you."

Then, one of my friends, Barbara came over and said, "Evie, great speech. Let's have a drink!"

Oh gosh, I thought to myself. I had already

promised Ponchie, and after running out on him with lunch, I didn't want to do that again. But if Barbara wasn't enough, two of my other friends walked up saying the same thing.

Finally, I said, "Why don't we all go to the lounge and we can all have a drink together."

Everyone agreed that that would be fun.

"Okay," I said. "But, I'll meet you all there because I have to get this basket up to my room." The Federation had given me a wonderful huge gift basket as appreciation for me being there.

Ponchie said, "I'll help you take the basket. I know it's heavy." He grabbed the basket, walked me to my room, placed the basket down, and we went right back down to the lounge.

At that time, Ponchie still had a lot of vision. So, he was able to arrange the chairs to keep everyone together. And as he arranged the chairs, he set it up so that I would be sitting across from him.

I thought that was very interesting. I'd met Ponchie before at other conventions, but there seemed to be just a little shift in the way he was acting toward me.

But for a few hours, we all sat together,

talking and laughing about the convention. While we were there, Ponchie never missed the opportunity to ask me a question -- it became obvious that he was trying to find out as much as he could about me.

When the lounge was finally closing, we all said goodnight and goodbye since most of us had flights leaving the next day. And, I told Ponchie that I had a great time hanging out with him.

Then, just days after I returned home, I received an email from him. And after that, we kept communicating that way. He'd email me, I'd send him inspirational quotes. It was just casual conversation, at first. And then, he told me that I should come visit him.

At first, I told myself absolutely not. This guy was younger than me and I wasn't sure if he knew my age. But then, I started talking to him about my birthday party.

My 70th birthday was coming up and though I didn't know exactly what I was going to be doing, I knew I was going to do something absolutely fabulous. But at that point, I talked about my birthday because I wanted to give Ponchie hints that I was older than him. I wanted to see if that mattered.

But, Ponchie didn't seem to care. In fact, he just kept telling me that I needed to come and visit him. I would joke with him and tell him to come and visit me, but while I was saying that, that's not what I wanted. Even though I have a separate entrance to my apartment, it was right off the garage and everyone would be able to see me with Ponchie.

And I knew that soon everybody would be calling him my new man and I didn't want that. What I really wanted was for Ponchie and I to develop a wholesome friendship.

Well, time passed and then in July, 2012 we were back at the national convention. I couldn't even get there good before Ponchie was emailing me – "When are you arriving, Evie? I can't wait to see you!"

It turned out that we were able to spend a lot of time together at that convention. Between lunch and dinner, and then the time when several of us hung out in Alecea's suite, we had a good time. And once we left, Ponchie and I still kept in touch.

By this time, though, I was in full planning

for my birthday. Victor and I talked about having a party at the House of Blues. He was thinking that we could go to the show and then afterward, have a huge, private party.

That had sounded like a good idea at first. But then, I contacted my siblings and no one really seemed to be all that interested or excited. They had all kinds of questions -- like where to stay, how were they going to get around. My birthday was beginning to feel like a real challenge and I began to wonder why was I wasting all of my time and energy on trying to prepare a birthday for me and my family in North Carolina didn't make a commitment.

That was when I told Victor that the House of Blues wasn't going to work. Not with my siblings. For them to spend money...I just knew they weren't going to do it and all the planning and worrying was going to be a big headache for me.

I told my son, "I just really want to enjoy my 70th birthday."

And that was the truth. All my life, I had been doing, giving, giving, doing, hardship, trials, tribulations. My life was good now. I was finally in a very good place and I wanted to do something that was just going to be just for me.

"Okay," Victor said, "So what are you going to do?"

I didn't have the answer then, but in a few weeks I did.

I was going to go on a cruise!

I told everyone about the cruise -- and my siblings weren't interested in that either. But then, I narrowed it down to my friends who were most likely to support me.

I told Judy, my best friend and her husband and they told me to count them in. Judy had never been on a cruise and she was excited.

I asked another friend, Yvonne, who was always there for me, especially during that time when I was going through that heartache with Theodore. And she told me to definitely count her in.

And then, I asked Ponchie!

I asked him straight out. "Would you be interested in going with me to celebrate my birthday on a cruise?"

"Count me in!" he said with no hesitation.

"Are you sure?"

"Count me in! I'd love to do this for you."

So, I sent him all of them the information for the cruise and right away, everyone responded. They put up their deposit money, got their passports in order, and we were on a roll -- for my 70th birthday on a cruise.

The night before the cruise, when they'd all arrived in California, we all stayed at the Beverly Hilton. It was a room that I had reserved for myself when I first began planning for my birthday and I wasn't sure what I was going to do. But they enjoyed being in that historical hotel and all of us were excited with anticipation of what the next days would bring.

The morning of the cruise, Victor, Brenda and the kids came over and we had breakfast together before our group left for the ship in Long Beach.

Just boarding the ship gave me such great feelings, but I had no idea how much of a good time I was going to have. That eight-days, seven nights cruise was one of the most memorable occasions of my life.

We docked in the ports of Puerto Vallarta and Cabo San Lucas and I got to explore those cities as well as when we were on the ship, I could do whatever I wanted to do. We went to the shows, we had great dinners. I even spent one full day at the spa -- it was nothing but laughter and good times. . . all for me.

There were no demands on me, I didn't have to answer to anyone, it was all about me. And the best part -- we were all there together, we connected, we got along so well. I felt so loved and cared for during that time. And it was a great opportunity for me to reflect back on my life.

I'd been through so much, from growing up on the plantation to finally finding my own way. Then, the challenges of marriage, the heartbreak of divorce, and the devastating prognosis for my eyesight.

But on the other hand, there had been a lot of joy: raising Victor and seeing him grow into the wonderful man that he was today, working with the Federation and being able to make a difference in so many people's lives.

Yes, there had been tragedies in my life, but at the same time, I'd never lost sight of my ambition. I was determined to succeed in spite of. So, I don't focus on the tragedies, rather, the seven decades of triumphs. And the greatest triumphant was that I had prevailed. I was 70 and on top of the world.

I was 70 and I was free. Of everything that had once held me back. And so, on my 70th birthday, as I cruised around with the people who loved me and whom I loved, I could finally and honestly say, "Free at last, free at last, thank God Almighty, Ever Lee Hairston was free at last!"

I am filled with hope, energy and love by participating in the National Federation of the Blind. Because my contributions make a difference to me and to others, I can celebrate the realizations of my dreams with my Federation family

And certainly live the life I want.

If you enjoyed Blind Ambition,
you'll love the riveting memoir

Against All Odds
From the Projects to the Penthouse

By Mahisha Dellinger

*(Enjoy this Sneak Peek)*

# Introduction

I've always known I was destined for great things. Don't ask me how I knew. I just did. It definitely couldn't have been my environment. After all, the mean streets of Sacramento can shatter anyone's dreams. In fact, my Meadowview neighborhood was dubbed "Danger Island" and although it was nestled between the affluent Pocket/Green haven area and lower middle class, Mack Road, it was not a place you wanted to be caught outside after dark.

I definitely didn't have the support at home. It's not that my family didn't believe in me and want more, but my mother was working so hard – and so long – that dreams (hers and mine) took a back seat.

However, I knew that I wouldn't allow someone else to write my story. I knew that my story was bigger than the impoverished streets I called home. And now, as my company, CURLS LLC, boasts its best year to date, I look back and reflect on where I've been and where I'm going.

I'm hoping that my story will inspire others to take their own journeys, to not let their pasts dictate their future, to go for their dreams and not let anything or anyone get in their way. While my story may be deemed a rags to riches tale, it's bigger than that. So much bigger. It's about an ordinary girl who decided she was capable of extraordinary things. It's about a woman who took all the obstacles tossed in her path of life and used them as stepping-stones to bigger and better things.

I truly have come from humble beginnings and as I worked my way up through the rigors of corporate America, the ups and downs of being an entrepreneur, the frustrations of trying to maintain a proper work-family balance, I've learned some valuable lessons. They are lessons that I share with you in the coming pages. From the pitfalls to the pinnacles, I bare it all.

Now, as my company – which started from my kitchen – is poised to post-record sales, I'm sharing my journey. Not only of how I overcame an impoverished background to pursue my passion, but also of how I went from just dreaming to doing. With valuable, applicable tips, it is my hope that after reading, the entrepreneurial spirit within you will be awakened.

My story can be your story. And if you walk away with nothing else, I hope that you'll understand my motto: When you wake up in the morning you have two choices - go back to sleep and dream your dreams, or get up and chase your dreams.

I choose the latter. What will your choice be?


*Mahisha*

# Chapter 1
## A Tale of Two Worlds

I'm not supposed to be here.

At least that's what the statistics said. According to all the studies, and the declarations of negative people in my life, if I did survive my gang-riddled neighborhood, it would be unwed with several children by my side, a dead-end, low-paying job, and a future that lacked hope. That's what the statistics said.

But I had a different ending for my story.
I never have settled for the norm. Even as a little girl, from a broken home, I knew that my destiny was greater than my existence. After all, I'd survived abuse, and my life had been spared more times than I could count.

Given my background, I could've easily become that sassy, tell-you-off, around- the-way girl who ran with the dope boys and held her own in the streets. Quite the contrary, though, I was about as close to perfection as you could get in a child.

With flopping pigtails and a smile that melted

everyone I met, people in the neighborhood knew that I wasn't like the rest of the girls. From a very young age, I was a very self-motivated, independent, and simply, an easy child to raise. I never got in trouble (I would occasionally mouth off, but my mother was quick to pop me in my mouth to get me back in line). I was where I was supposed to be, when I was supposed to be there.

However, one day, I wasn't where I was supposed to be - at John Sloat Elementary School. To this day, I believe my mother's boyfriend, Willie, is to blame.

My daily routine was the same - my mom left for work at 7 a.m. I got myself up, dressed, and off to school by 8:30 a.m. Willie was always the last person to leave before me, he knew that the garage was my only way out. I didn't have a house key (my brother did because he always made it home from school before me, so I didn't need one). Willie knew that I exited through the kitchen into the garage, manually lifting the exterior garage door. This day was like no other, except when I went to lift the wooden garage door to head to school, it was locked. I had already locked the door to the house so I couldn't get out. I was stuck!

**Want more? Order your copy now!**
**Available Everywhere!**
**And make sure you sign our mailing list at**
**www.BrownGirlsBooks.com**

Made in the USA
Middletown, DE
24 April 2020